Adobe Photoshop 2024 User GuideBook

The Complete Step-by- Step Tutorial for Beginners on Adobe Photoshop 2024, Including Advanced Techniques, Latest Features, and Basic Photo Editing Tools

Curtis
Campbell

Disclaimer

The information in this book is based on personal experience and anecdotal evidence. Although the author has made every attempt to achieve an accuracy of the information gathered in this book, they make no representation or warranties concerning the accuracy or completeness of the contents of this book. Your circumstances may not be suited to some illustrations in this book.

The author disclaims any liability arising directly or indirectly from the use of this book. Readers are encouraged to seek Medical. Accounting, legal, or professional help when required.

This guide is for informational purposes only, and the author does not accept any responsibilities for any liabilities resulting from the use of this information. While every attempt has been made to verify the information provided here, the author cannot assume any responsibility for errors, inaccuracies or omission.

Printed in the United States of America

Table of Contents

INTRODUCTION

Welcome to the complete guidebook to using Adobe Photoshop 2024. Whether you're a beginner looking to learn the basics or a seasoned pro seeking to master the latest features, this guide has something for you.

In the following pages, we'll cover everything from the redesigned user interface to enhanced editing tools like the new Select Subject and Sky Replacement functions.

You'll learn how to edit photos like a pro with features like Content-Aware Fill and improved Camera Raw. We'll also walk through creating complex composites, manipulating 3D imagery, and using powerful automation to speed up workflows.

With tips and tutorials for users of all levels, this guidebook will help you get the most out of Photoshop 2024 and take your photo editing skills to new heights.

Let's get started!

CHAPTER ONE

Review: Adobe Photoshop 2024

Adobe has released Photoshop 2024, the latest version of its industry-standard photo editing software. Photoshop 2024 brings some of the most substantial improvements and additions to the program in years, with major upgrades to performance, new AI capabilities, and enhanced creative workflows.

As the market leader in image editing and graphic design, each new release of Photoshop is highly anticipated by creative professionals and hobbyists alike. Version 25 continues Adobe's tradition of releasing major updates every couple of years.

This review will examine Photoshop 2024's new features, UI changes, system performance, and overall capabilities. While the core tools remain familiar, Adobe has injected machine learning throughout the software to augment workflows. The most notable improvements are in workflow automation, AI-powered selection tools, new compositing capabilities, and cloud collaboration features.

Interface and Features

- ## Streamlined UI and UX

The user interface (UI) of Photoshop 2024 remains centered around familiar tools and panels, but it has been refined for better convenience. Menu options have been reorganized for more logical workflows, and panel management has been improved. One particular upgrade is the ability to condense all docked panels into a single tabbed bar, decluttering the workspace.

While experienced users will notice the changes, the UI improvements are aimed at new users. Adobe has focused on onboarding new Photoshop users with prompted walkthroughs, contextual help menus, and built-in tutorials. This makes the software more approachable for beginners.

- **Lens Blur**

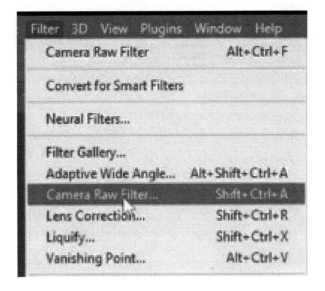

The Lens Blur panel under the **Filter > Camera Raw** menu in Photoshop provides a powerful way to add realistic optical blur effects and beautiful bokeh to your photos.

To use this feature, check the **"Apply"** box and adjust the **Blur Amount** slider to control the strength of the effect. You can also select different bokeh styles to change the look of the blurred highlights. The **"Boost"** slider offers further fine-tuning of the bokeh intensity.

Alternatively, you can manually set the focal range for ultimate control over where the blur is applied.

This makes it easy to achieve the perfect depth-of-field effect.

An exciting addition to Lens Blur is the depth map visualization. Check the **"Visualize Depth"** box to see a synthetic depth map that uses 3D depth estimation to represent the distances in your image. Adjusting the focal range in this mode is very intuitive, with a white overlay showing what's currently in focus. You can even refine the depth map using the dedicated focus and blur brushes.

The Lens Blur feature provides an intuitive way to add realistic depth-of-field effects to your photos in Photoshop. The depth map visualization takes the precision even further.

- **The New Era of Object Removal**

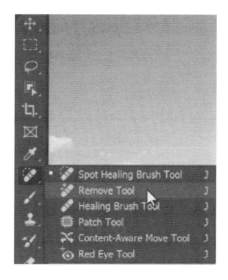

The tedious task of manually brushing over objects for removal in Photoshop is outdated.

The latest 2024 version introduces the revolutionary **Remove Tool**, which takes object removal to new heights in terms of efficiency and speed.

To use it, simply draw a loop around the object you want to eliminate. Photoshop's intelligent algorithms will automatically connect the endpoints and fill in the selected area with appropriate image content, removing the object as if by magic.

This tool streamlines the removal process, saving users time and effort. No longer is precise, painstaking brushwork needed to cover unwanted objects in a photo. With the innovative Remove Tool, object removal is faster and easier than ever before.

The new capabilities usher in an exciting new era of efficient photo editing in Photoshop. The Remove Tool represents a major leap forward, fundamentally changing the way users can erase objects from images. This revolution in removal technology will undoubtedly become an indispensable part of every Photoshop user's workflow.

- ## **Getting Creative with Parametric Filters**

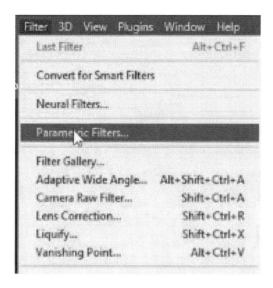

The latest Photoshop beta version 25.2 offers an exciting array of parametric filters under **Filter > Parametric Filters** to spark your creative vision.

You can now easily apply stunning effects like Oil Painting, Glitch, and Scratch Photo to images. These filters provide extensive customization through different parameter options, empowering you to find the perfect look. Make sure to try out the diverse presets too and discover inspiring styles tailored to your needs.

- **An Improved Contextual Task Bar**

Photoshop's Contextual Task Bar just got even more robust. The new **"Pin bar position"** option lets you save your customized bar setup, so the tools you want are always at hand, even after restarting Photoshop. This saves you time and effort.

Masking and cropping also benefit from enhanced features in the **Contextual Task Bar**. New buttons provide quick access to key functions while working in these modes. Most notably, the revolutionary Generative Expand feature leverages AI to intelligently expand your selections and crops naturally.

- **The Power of AI with New Generative Fill**

The 2024 release of Photoshop ushers in the era of Generative AI for commercial use. A highlight is the magical new Generative Fill feature, empowered by text prompts in over 100 languages.

Simply make a selection, type a text description, and watch as Photoshop intelligently fills the area.

The AI matches lighting, perspective, and depth for incredibly natural results.

The Generative Fill layer stores multiple fill variations, giving you the flexibility to pick the ideal outcome. Remarkably, it works seamlessly on photos, illustrations, and drawings.

You can even utilize Generative Fill to effortlessly remove unwanted elements from images.

This AI technology in Photoshop massively expands creative potential. Generative Fill puts the power of text-to-image generation directly into your workflows, saving vast amounts of time while bringing visions to life. Welcome to the future of intelligent, automated creativity with Photoshop 2024.

- **Revolutionizing Cropping with Generative Expand**

Photoshop's new Generative Expand capability is an absolute game-changer for intelligently expanding cropped images.

When using the Crop Tool, select **"Generative Expand"** from the dropdown menu. Now, changing the photo's aspect ratio triggers Photoshop to magically generate content to fill transparent areas, powered by AI.

The results are jaw-dropping compared to old Content-Aware Fill methods. Photoshop synthesizes stunning, realistic image extensions you'd swear were present in the original photo.

- ## **Managing Generative AI Resources Credits**

Plan	Monthly generative credits
Creative Cloud All Apps	1,000
Creative Cloud Single App • Illustrator, InDesign, Photoshop, Premiere Pro, After Effects, Audition, Animate, Adobe Dreamweaver, Adobe Stock, Photography 1TB	500

Creative Cloud Single App
 	
• Creative Cloud Photography 20GB:
 	
    • Subscribers before November 1, 2023
    • Subscribers after November 1, 2023
	
	250
	100

Creative Cloud Single App • Lightroom	100
Creative Cloud Single App • InCopy, Substance 3D Collection, Substance 3D Texturing, Acrobat Pro	25

Adobe has implemented a credit system to optimize computational resource usage for Generative AI features.

Depending on your Photoshop subscription plan, you'll receive a monthly credit allocation that prioritizes processing speed. If you exceed your credits, Generative AI will still function but may run slower.

Additional credits can be purchased starting at $4.99 for 100 credits by upgrading your subscription. This allows flexibility in boosting credits as needed for faster processing.

The credits provide sensible management of Generative AI resources. With your included monthly credits and ability to buy more, you can efficiently utilize these computationally intensive features. The credit system ensures optimal performance while giving you control over spending.

- **Promoting Trust with Content Credentials AI Tag**

Photoshop 2024 introduces Content Credentials - AI-generated tags automatically added to created images for transparency in the digital age.

The tags provide key details on an image's origins, helping curb misinformation by giving proper credit and clarity. You can customize shared credentials and enable/disable specific info.

To use Content Credentials, go to **Window > Content Credentials** and click **"Enable."**

The **Preview** shows how images will display with credentials.

To view any photo's Content Credentials, go to **contentcredentials.org/verify** and upload the image.

Photoshop's Content Credentials promote trust by tagging generated images with authoritative details. As visual misinformation spreads rapidly online, this AI feature brings accountability, giving creators credit and providing vital context for their work. With custom controls, you can share images ethically and transparently.

- **Verdict**

Adobe Photoshop 2024 delivers substantive upgrades and quality-of-life improvements that will please both new and experienced Photoshop users. The focus on AI, automation, and collaboration signals where Adobe sees the future headed.

While the subscription cost is still an impediment for hobbyists, Photoshop remains the undisputed industry standard in photo manipulation and compositing. For professionals who rely on it for client work, the upgrades in Photoshop 2024 make the update worth considering. This release maintains Photoshop's edge as the foremost image editing and design application.

Getting Started with Adobe Photoshop

Download

Before downloading Photoshop, make sure your computer meets the minimum system requirements:

- **Operating System:** Windows 10 64-bit or later, or macOS Big Sur 11.0 or later
- **RAM:** 8 GB minimum (16 GB recommended)
- **Storage:** 10 GB free space on the hard drive
- **Display:** 1280x800 screen resolution

Newer computers produced in the last couple of years will likely meet these specs. Photoshop also benefits greatly from a dedicated GPU graphics card.

Downloading Photoshop

- Go to the Adobe Photoshop homepage **www.adobe.com/photoshop**.
- Click the blue **"Buy Now"** or **"Try Now"** button.

- Choose between Photoshop subscription plans. The Single App plan provides just Photoshop for $263.88/year.
- Click **"Add to Cart"** and checkout with your payment method.
- On the following page, click the **"Download Now"** button. This downloads the Adobe Creative Cloud app.
- Open the downloaded Creative Cloud app installer and follow the prompts to install it.
- Sign into Creative Cloud using your new Adobe ID account credentials.
- Photoshop will now be available for you to download and install!

Installing Photoshop

- In the Creative Cloud app, click the **"Install"** button under the Photoshop banner.
- Choose the language you want for the Photoshop interface.
- Read through the licensing agreement. Click **"Accept"** once you agree to the terms.

- Select whether you want to enable **Font Syncing**. This syncs any new fonts you install between your computers.
- Click **"Start"** to begin the installation process.
- Photoshop may take several minutes to fully install. The progress will be displayed.
- Once completed, Photoshop is ready to launch. The app icon will appear in your computer's **Start Menu/Dock**. Opening it for the first time may take a bit longer as Photoshop initializes.

Troubleshooting Tips

If you encounter issues downloading, installing, or opening Photoshop, here are some troubleshooting tips:

- Check that your computer meets the minimum system requirements outlined above. Upgrading RAM or GPU may help.
- Disable any antivirus or firewall temporarily to allow the Adobe apps to install smoothly, then re-enable after.

- Update your operating system, graphics drivers, and Creative Cloud app to the latest versions for compatibility.

- Try uninstalling and re-downloading Photoshop if the installation fails or the app seems corrupted.

- Consult Adobe's forums or contact Customer Service for additional support if needed.

With Photoshop 2024 installed you can now start editing photos and creating artwork. Don't be intimidated by the vast toolkit - focus on learning the basics first.

Installing Current Updates

Photoshop updates include a mix of new capabilities, optimizations, and fixes that improve the overall software. Some updates add new creative tools or options, while others focus on speed boosts and stability. Updating frequently prevents bugs and ensures maximum compatibility with operating systems, graphics cards, and other programs.

It only takes a few minutes to check for and download updates. Follow the steps below to get Photoshop updated to the latest version.

Check for Updates

- Open the **Creative Cloud** desktop app.
- Click on the Photoshop banner.
- Navigate to the **Settings** tab (gear icon).
- Under **App Updates**, it will show the current Photoshop version installed.
- Click the **Check for App Updates** button.
- Creative Cloud will communicate with Adobe's servers to see if any new Photoshop updates are available to download.
- If an update is detected, the new version number will display under Available Updates along with an Update button.

Download the Update

- Click the Update button next to Photoshop to begin the download.
- A progress bar will fill as the update files get downloaded from Adobe's servers.
- Download speeds will vary based on your internet connection. Faster broadband speeds will complete the download quicker.
- Once the download is finished, you'll see a notification that it's ready to install.

Install the Update

- In **Creative Cloud**, click the Install button shown next to Photoshop under **Available Updates**.
- A panel will open showing the installation progress. Do not disrupt the computer during installation.

- Photoshop may need to close and relaunch to complete the update installation if it is open. Save your work first.
- Allow a few minutes for the update process to fully complete. The progress bar will fill to 100%.
- When finished, Photoshop will relaunch at the latest version.
- Check **Help > About Photoshop** to confirm the new version number installed.

Following these steps whenever Adobe releases new updates will ensure you stay up-to-date.

CHAPTER TWO

Understanding the Photoshop 2024 Interface

With a vast array of tools and capabilities, the Photoshop 2024 interface can seem daunting to new users. This guide will walk you through the key parts of the interface to help you quickly get up to speed.

The Menu Bar

The Menu Bar runs along the top of the Photoshop window and contains dropdown menus for all the main functions and tools. Let's take a look at each one:

- **File Menu**

The File menu contains options related to opening, saving, exporting, and closing files. Key options include:

Open - Open an existing image file.

New - Create a new blank file to work on.

Save and Save As - Save the current file.

Export - Export and save the file in different file formats.

Close - Close the current file.

- **Edit Menu**

The Edit menu provides options to edit and modify images. Common tools here:

Undo - Undo recent changes.

Redo - Redo changes that were undone.

Cut, Copy, Paste - Basic editing tools to cut, copy and paste selections.

Transform - Options to scale, rotate, skew, distort, and perspective warp selections.

Image Size - Change canvas size and image resolution.

- **Image Menu**

The Image menu contains adjustments and editing tools related to the whole image:

Image Rotation - Rotate and flip the canvas and image.

Image Size - Change image dimensions and resolution.

Canvas Size - Change canvas size.

Crop - Crop the image.

Trim - Trim away transparent edges.

- **Layer Menu**

The Layer menu handles layers and lets you:

New layers - Create new layers.

Duplicate layers - Duplicate existing layers.

Delete layers - Delete the selected layers.

Merge layers - Merge selected layers into one.

Layer Style - Apply styles like drop shadow.

- **Type Menu**

The Type menu deals with working with text layers:

Horizontal/Vertical Type - Create new text layers.

Convert to Shape - Convert text into vector shapes.

Type Layers - Manage and work with text layers.

Font and Paragraph settings - Change text formatting.

- **Select Menu**

Use the Select menu to make selections and masks:

Select All - Select everything on the canvas.

Deselect - Deselect any active selections.

Reselect - Reselect previous selection.

Select Inverse - Invert the selection.

Select Color Range - Make a selection based on color.

- **Filter Menu**

The Filter menu contains all the filter effects you can apply:

Blur - Blur and smooth areas.

Sharpen - Sharpen details.

Distort - Distort, pinch, and polarize the image.

Noise - Add or remove noise.

Filter Gallery - Browse all filters.

- **View Menu**

The View menu lets you control the preview zoom and layout:

Actual Pixels - View at 100% size.

Fit on Screen - Fit the image to the screen.

Zoom In/Out - Manual zoom controls.

Layout - Change to a single window or multiple window layouts.

- **Window Menu**

Use the Window menu to manage panels and workspaces:

Workspace - Choose between default workspaces like Essentials.

Tools - Open tools like brush tools.

Properties - Open panels like layers.

Arrange - Organize panel positions.

- **Help Menu**

Finally, the Help menu contains:

Photoshop Help - Search for help articles and resources.

Updates - Check for software updates.

About Photoshop - View application details.

- **Toolbars**

Below the Menu Bar are preset toolbars you can toggle on and off containing shortcuts to common tools:

Tools - Tools like selection, crop, and brush.

Colors - Foreground/background colors and swatches.

Layers - Layers toggles.

Modes - Image blending modes.

History - Undo/redo history.

- **Panels**

Panels are movable windows containing sets of related tools and functions. Examples include:

Layers - Manage layers.

Adjustments - Color, lighting, and contrast adjustments.

Brushes - Manage and customize brushes.

Actions - Manage reusable actions.

Properties - View properties for selected objects.

You can access panels through the Window menu.

- **Contextual Task Bar**

This is the task bar located at the lower mid part of the interface and it can be moved or pinned to another location on your workspace.

The Options Bar

The Options Bar is an essential component of the Adobe Photoshop interface located just below the main menu bar. It displays context-sensitive options that relate to the active tool, allowing you to configure the tool's settings and modify how it operates.

Accessing the Options Bar

The Options Bar is visible whenever you have a document open in Photoshop. It will change based on the active tool selected.

To access it:

Select a tool from the Tools panel on the left side of the interface. This can include selection tools like the Rectangular Marquee Tool or editing tools like the Paint Brush.

Look below the main menu bar to see the Options Bar appear with settings for the chosen tool.

Key Options Bar Features

The Options Bar contains various controls and options that may include:

- **Tool Settings**

The most common settings and configurations for the selected tool. For example, the Paint Brush tool shows options for Brush Tip Shape, Size, Hardness, and Spacing.

- **Brush/Tool Presets**

A dropdown menu to select preset configurations for brushes and tools. Switch between different brush types or tool settings.

- **Blend Modes**

A dropdown to change the blend mode and determine how your edits blend with the image below. Modes like Overlay and Multiply have different effects.

- **Opacity/Flow**

Sliders to adjust opacity and flow for painting or editing strength. Lower opacity for transparent effects.

- **Layer Options**

Options like lock transparency to constrain edits to a single layer.

- **Swatch Selectors**

Color swatches for choosing foreground and background colors.

Customizing the Options Bar

You can customize the Options Bar to better suit your workflow:

- **Add More Options**

Right-click on the Options Bar.

Choose Customize from the menu.

Check the boxes to add or remove options from the Options Bar.

- **Reset Default Options**

Right-click on the Options Bar.

Select Restore Defaults to reset to the tool's original Options Bar settings.

- **Move Position**

Click the gray double arrow icon on the far left side of the Options Bar.

Drag it up or down to reposition the Options Bar.

- **Quickly Hide/Show**

Right-click on the Options Bar and toggle Hide Options Bar to quickly minimize a distracting Options Bar.

Understanding how to leverage the Options Bar is a key skill for Photoshop 2024 proficiency.

Panels

Panels are located on the right side of the Photoshop interface in vertical groups. To open a panel:

- ✓ Go to Window in the main menu.
- ✓ Hover over the panel name and click to open it.
- ✓ Dock the panel on the right side.
- ✓ You can also undock panels and move them around your workspace. Let's look at the key panels:

Layers Panel

The Layers panel allows you to manage all the layers in your document:

- ✓ View all layers and arrange layer order.
- ✓ Adjust opacity and blend modes.

✓ Organize with groups and naming.

✓ Add layer styles like drop shadows.

To use the Layers panel:

✓ Open the Layers panel.

✓ Click and drag layers to reorder them.

✓ Use the options across the bottom to control layers.

Channels Panel

The Channels panel lets you adjust individual color channels:

✓ View the composite RGB channel.

✓ Adjust individual R, G, and B channels.

✓ Use channels to make selections.

To view channels:

✓ Open the Channels panel.

✓ Click on the eye icon to view different channels.

✓ Click Save selection to save a channel as a selection.

Paths Panel

The Paths panel allows you to work with vector paths:

- ✓ Create new paths with the Pen tool.
- ✓ Make selections from paths.
- ✓ Load and save pre-made paths.

To create a path:

- ✓ Select the Pen tool.
- ✓ Draw out a path by adding anchor points.
- ✓ Adjust the path shape with direction lines.
- ✓ Save the path in the Paths panel.

Info Panel

The Info panel displays details about your selections, tools, and documents:

- ✓ View selection information like size, bounds, and color.
- ✓ See tool settings like brush size and opacity.
- ✓ View document details like name, size, and color mode.

To use the Info panel:

- ✓ Open the Info panel.
- ✓ Hover or click over elements to view information.

Color Panel

The Color panel lets you manage color swatches, hexadecimal codes, and your color picker:

- ✓ View and select preset swatches.
- ✓ Enter hexadecimal color codes.
- ✓ Use the color picker to sample colors.
- ✓ Create and save new swatch libraries.

To sample a color:

- ✓ Open the Color panel.
- ✓ Click on the color picker icon.
- ✓ Hover over any color in your document to sample it.

Adjustments Panel

Use the Adjustments panel to tweak image colors, lighting, and contrast:

- ✓ Apply adjustments like Levels, Curves, and Hue/Saturation.
- ✓ Make tonal corrections and color grading.
- ✓ Adjust brightness, contrast, and exposure.

To adjust Levels:

- ✓ Open the Adjustments panel.
- ✓ Click on the Levels icon.
- ✓ Drag the sliders to adjust shadows, highlights, and midtones.

History Panel

The History panel lets you revert actions and undo mistakes:

- ✓ Step back through recent edits and actions.
- ✓ Create snapshots to save certain states.
- ✓ Revert to a previous point.

To use the History panel:

- ✓ Open the History panel.
- ✓ Click on a previous state to revert.
- ✓ Click the snapshot icon to save any state.

The Document Window

When you first open or create a document in Photoshop, you'll be presented with the document window. This contains:

Image/Canvas Area

The center of the window shows the image itself on the canvas:

- ✓ The canvas is the working area where you'll apply edits.
- ✓ Images are displayed on top of the canvas.
- ✓ The canvas can extend beyond the viewable area.

To move around the canvas:

- ✓ Click and drag the Hand tool to pan across the image.
- ✓ Use the Zoom tool to zoom in and out.

Navigation Controls

Around the canvas are navigation controls:

✓ Zoom In/Out tools to magnify the view.

✓ The hand tool moves the canvas.

✓ Rotation tools and scrubby zoom.

✓ Reset Zoom and Fit to Screen buttons.

To zoom in:

✓ Select the Zoom In tool.

✓ Click on the area you want to magnify.

✓ Repeat to continue zooming in.

Zoom Level

The zoom level appears in the bottom left:

✓ Displays the current zoom as a percentage.

✓ 100% represents actual pixels.

✓ Higher percentages zoom in further.

To set a specific zoom level:

✓ Go to View > Zoom In.

✓ Select a preset percentage zoom.

View Menu

The View menu contains display options:

✓ **Proof Colors** - Preview different color profiles.

✓ **Extras** - Show overlays like guides and grids.

✓ **Show/Hide elements** - Toggle visibility of tools, panels, etc.

To show a grid overlay:

✓ Go to View > Show > Grid.

✓ Adjust grid settings in Preferences.

Customizing the Workspace

One of the easiest ways to customize your Photoshop workspace is by changing the overall panel layout. Photoshop offers preset layouts that optimize panels for different types of workflows. Here's how to change the panel layout:

Click on Window in the Menu bar and select Workspace.

Select the desired panel layout from the menu. Some top options include:

Essentials: Displays only the most commonly used panels.

Default: The default Photoshop panel layout.

Photography: Optimized for photographic editing.

Graphic and Web: Ideal for web/graphic design work.

Motion: Tailored for video and animation workflows.

Painting: Displays panels suited for digital painting.

The selected layout will rearrange your workspace panels automatically. Try a few different layouts to find one suited to your needs.

✓ **Collapsing/Expanding Panels**

To conserve screen space, you can collapse panels you aren't currently using. Here's how:

Locate the panel menu icon in the top-right corner of the panel. It appears as three small lines.

Click the icon to collapse the panel down to just the panel name. This removes the panel from the screen while keeping it easily accessible.

To expand a collapsed panel, simply click its name to restore it to the full panel view.

Collapsing panels declutter your workspace and allow you to maximize the screen space for the tools you're currently using.

✓ **Docking/Undocking Panels**

Photoshop allows you to dock panels together into neat panel groups, or undock panels to move them freely around your workspace.

To dock a panel:

Click and drag the panel title bar toward another panel group until a blue shaded area appears, then release. The panel will snap into place with the group.

To undock a panel:

Click and drag the panel tab and move your mouse away from the panel group. Once the blue shaded area disappears, release to undock the panel.

You can now move the free-floating panel anywhere on the screen.

Docking organizes related panels together while undocking lets you fully customize placement. Use a combination of docking and undocking to create a unique layout.

✓ **Creating Custom Workspaces**

For extensive customization, you can save your optimized panel layouts as custom workspaces that can be easily accessed later.

To save a custom workspace:

Get your workspace layout exactly as desired, with your preferred panels open and arranged.

Go to **Window > Workspace > New Workspace**.

Name your custom workspace and click Save.

To access a saved custom workspace:

Select Window > Workspace > [Your Workspace Name].

Photoshop will reopen with the custom workspace applied.

Saving custom layouts makes it easy to instantly switch between optimized workspaces for different editing tasks.

✓ **Resetting the Default Workspace**

If your extensive workspace customizing leads to a cluttered mess, you can always reset Photoshop back to the default panel layout:

Navigate to Window > Workspace > Reset [Name of Current Workspace].

Photoshop will prompt you to confirm - click Reset.

The default Photoshop workspace layout will be restored.

Resetting to the default clears out any disorganized panel arrangements and gives you a clean slate to start customizing again.

Navigating the Interface

Zooming in and out is one of the most common Photoshop navigation techniques for viewing specific image areas in detail. Here are the different ways to zoom in and zoom out:

To zoom in: Click the Zoom tool in the toolbar, then click on the area of the image you want to magnify. Each click zooms in closer.

To zoom out: Hold the Alt (PC) or Option (Mac) key and click with the Zoom tool. Each click zooms out further.

Use the Zoom Level drop-down menu at the bottom of the toolbar to select a specific zoom percentage.

Click View > Zoom In or View > Zoom Out in the menu bar.

Use the keyboard shortcuts Ctrl+"+" (PC) or Cmd "+" (Mac) to zoom in and Ctrl+"-" (PC) or Cmd "-" (Mac) to zoom out.

Scrub the mouse scroll wheel forward or backward to smoothly zoom in and out.

✓ **Using the Hand Tool**

The Hand tool allows you to grab and pan around the image for easy navigation when zoomed in. To use it:

Select the Hand tool from the toolbar (or use the keyboard shortcut H).

Click and drag with the Hand tool to pan the image in any direction.

Release the mouse when the desired image area is in view.

Using the Hand tool prevents you from accidentally making edits while panning at high zoom levels. Get comfortable panning so you can easily access all parts of a zoomed image.

✓ **Changing Screen Modes**

Photoshop offers different screen modes to control the interface view. The three main modes are:

Standard Screen Mode

This is the default standard Photoshop layout with toolbars and panels available. To enter Standard Screen Mode:

Click the arrow in the bottom-right corner of any panel to cycle through the mode options until Standard Screen Mode is displayed.

Or select **View > Screen Mode > Standard Screen Mode.**

Use this mode when you need to access the full Photoshop interface with all toolbars and panels open.

Full-Screen Mode

This mode fills the entire screen with just the image window, hiding all the interface extras. To enter Full Screen Mode:

Click the arrow in the bottom-right corner of any panel and select Full Screen Mode.

Or press the F key.

Full Screen Mode provides distraction-free viewing of the image you're editing.

Full Screen Mode with Menu Bar

This looks identical to Full Screen Mode but leaves the menu bar available at the top. To enter Full Screen Mode with Menu Bar:

Click the arrow in the bottom-right corner of any panel and select Full Screen Mode with Menu Bar.

Or press the Shift + F key.

This provides a good balance of interface simplicity while leaving menu options accessible.

CHAPTER THREE

Working with Documents

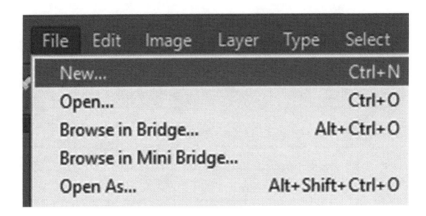

When launching Photoshop 2024, a welcome screen prompts you to make a new file, open an existing document, or use a template. Here's how to create a new PSD from scratch:

✓ Open Photoshop and select New... from the welcome screen. Alternatively, go to **File > New...** from the main menu.

✓ In the New Document window, name your file.

- ✓ Set your desired dimensions in pixels, inches, cm, etc.
- ✓ Choose the Resolution. 300 pixels/inch is recommended for print graphics; 72 pixels/inch for web.
- ✓ Select the Color Mode: RGB for digital media or CMYK for print design.
- ✓ Select either a white or transparent Background.
- ✓ Click Create and your new Photoshop document will open!

Preset Document Sizes

Rather than entering custom dimensions, you can choose from a range of preset document sizes:

- ✓ Select a preset size like Letter, Legal, Tabloid, A4, etc.
- ✓ Go to the Photo category to pick from standard photo print sizes.
- ✓ Film & Video presets are tailored for different display media.

- ✓ The Mobile category has sizes for designing apps and websites.
- ✓ There are Art & Illustration and Web presets as well.

Custom Document Size

To create a custom document size not listed in the presets:

- ✓ In the New Document window, change the Width and Height units to your desired measurement.
- ✓ Enter your custom Width and Height values.
- ✓ Set the Resolution, Color Mode, and Background as needed.
- ✓ Click Create.
- ✓ This allows complete control over the exact pixel or print dimensions for a PSD.

Opening Existing Documents

To open a Photoshop document already saved on your computer:

- ✓ Go to **File > Open...** or click **Open...** from the welcome screen.
- ✓ Navigate to the PSD file location and select it.
- ✓ Click Open.
- ✓ You can also open recent files from the File menu. Photoshop will launch the document with its layers, settings, etc. intact.

Saving Documents

Saving your work regularly is essential in Photoshop. To save in the native PSD format:

- ✓ Go to **File > Save** or **File > Save As...** The first time, use Save As to choose a file location and name.
- ✓ Keyboard shortcut: Ctrl + S on Windows or Command + S on Mac.

Photoshop (PSD) Format

PSD is the default Photoshop format that preserves all editing capabilities. Benefits include:

- ✓ Maintains layers, masks, transparency, text, and other features.

✓ Allows non-destructive editing of images.

✓ Saves Photoshop-specific data like brush strokes.

✓ Works seamlessly with other Adobe apps.

Other File Formats

To save or export in other formats like JPG, PNG, PDF, TIFF, etc.:

Go to **File > Export** or **Save As...**

Select the desired file format from the drop-down menu.

Adjust any format-specific options and click Save.

This creates a copy of your PSD in the chosen format. The original editable PSD remains intact.

Closing Documents

When finished working on a Photoshop document, close it by:

✓ Clicking the **X** in the upper corner of the document window.

✓ Going to **File > Close**.

✓ Pressing Ctrl + W in Windows or Command + W on a Mac.

✓ Save any changes before closing. Closing a document does not save automatically in Photoshop.

Managing Layers

A Photoshop document can contain multiple layers stacked on top of each other. Think of layers like sheets of transparent film. Each one holds a different element of your image. Working with layers rather than a single flattened image allows nondestructive editing and rearranging of design components.

Adding New Layers

Create a new blank layer:

- ✓ Click the Create a new layer icon at the bottom of the Layers panel.
- ✓ Go to **Layer > New > Layer**.
- ✓ Keyboard shortcut Ctrl + Shift + N (Win) / Cmd + Shift + N (Mac).
- ✓ Layers can also be created from pasting or importing images.

Selecting Layers

To edit, move, or modify a layer, you must first select it:

- ✓ Click the layer thumbnail in the Layers panel.
- ✓ Click the layer content in your document.
- ✓ Ctrl (Win) or Cmd (Mac) click multiple layers to select more than one.
- ✓ The active layer will be highlighted.

Deleting Layers

To delete a layer:

- ✓ Select the layer to delete.
- ✓ Drag it to the trash icon at the bottom of the Layers panel.
- ✓ Alternatively, right-click and select Delete Layer.

Duplicating Layers

Duplicate layers quickly using:

- ✓ Right-click on layer > Duplicate Layer
- ✓ Ctrl/Cmd + J
- ✓ Drag the layer thumbnail to Create a new layer icon
- ✓ This stacks a copy directly above the original.

Moving Layers

Click and drag a layer to reposition it vertically in the stacking order. Move up to bring it forward; down to send it backward.

Dragging Layers

To move a layer's content, use the Move tool:

- ✓ Select the layer.
- ✓ Choose the Move tool from the toolbar.
- ✓ Drag elements to the desired position.

Using the Layers Panel

Manage your layers via the Layers panel (Window > Layers):

- ✓ Organize, sort, and search layers.
- ✓ Hide, group, and lock layers.
- ✓ Adjust opacity and blending modes.
- ✓ Add layer styles like drop shadows.

Changing Layer Order

Rearrange layers vertically by dragging & dropping in the Layers panel. The top layers overlay those below.

Grouping Layers

Select multiple layers and group them:

- ✓ Click the Create a new group icon.
- ✓ Ctrl/Cmd + G

✓ This collapses the layers into a single group that can be moved as one unit.

Linking Layers

Linking layers maintain their relative positions when moving:

✓ Select layers to link.
✓ Click the chain icon to link.

Locking Layers

✓ Lock a layer to prevent accidental changes to its content:
✓ Click the empty box icon next to the layer to toggle the lock on/off.
✓ Locked layers remain visible but cannot be edited.

Blending Layers

Adjusting layer blend modes and opacity controls how content interacts. Experiment to create unique layered effects.

Adjusting Canvas Size

Access canvas size options by going to **Image >
Canvas Size**. This opens the Canvas Size dialog box.
From here you can enter precise values or use
dynamic controls to resize your canvas.

Increasing Canvas Size

To enlarge canvas space:

- ✓ Enter larger Width and Height values in the
  Canvas Size dialog box. Click OK.
- ✓ Alternatively, drag the handles of the canvas
  preview outward. Click OK to apply.
- ✓ New space will be added evenly to all edges
  by default. Drag edge arrows inward to offset.

Relative vs. Absolute Increase

Enlarge canvas by absolute pixels or relative
percent:

Absolute: Add specific Width/Height values in
pixels, inches, etc.

Relative: Choose a percent increase. 200% double canvas size.

Decreasing Canvas Size

To downsize and trim the canvas area:

- ✓ In the Canvas Size dialog box, adjust W and H to smaller values.
- ✓ Drag handles of canvas preview inward to desired crop size.
- ✓ Click OK to remove the exterior portion of the canvas.

Cropping the Canvas

Rather than resizing, crop to cut a section of the canvas out:

- ✓ Select your region for cropping with a marquee or lasso tool.
- ✓ Go to Image > Crop or press Ctrl/Cmd + Shift + C.
- ✓ The cropped area becomes your new canvas size.

CHAPTER FOUR

Selection Basics

A selection isolates a portion of an image, protecting just that area from changes. Any edits, effects, adjustments, etc. that you apply will only affect the selected area, not the entire image. This allows precise, focused editing.

Selections have soft or hard edges:

Soft-edged selections blend gradually outward from the selection border. These are useful for natural-looking refinements.

Hard-edged selections have a sharp, defined edge at the selection border. These are used for precise, geometric selections.

Visual cue - Marching Ants:

When an area is selected, Photoshop displays a moving dashed border called "marching ants". This animated border lets you see your selection.

Selecting Pixels, Shapes, or Objects

Photoshop 2024 offers several selection tools, each suited for different purposes:

Rectangular Marquee: Selects rectangular regions in an image

Elliptical Marquee: Selects oval or circular regions

Lasso: Freehand selection by tracing an area with a cursor

Polygonal Lasso: Select areas with straight-line segments

Magnetic Lasso: Snaps to edges as you draw a selection border

Quick Selection: Intelligent selection based on brush strokes over an area

Magic Wand: Selects similarly colored regions with one click

Color Range: Selects regions of an image based on color

Visualizing Selections (Marching Ants)

As mentioned above, Photoshop displays selections with an animated dashed line called marching ants. Here are some tips for working with the marching ants display:

Thickness indicates selection size - thicker ants equate to larger selections

Color determines selection type - default is white, but can be changed

Turn off/on by pressing Ctrl/Cmd + H

Display options adjust the appearance of the ants

Allows real-time visualization of your selection

✓ Soft vs Hard Edges

Selections can have a soft, feathered edge or a hard, sharp edge. Each is useful in different situations:

Soft edge:

Creates a gradual, natural blend at the selection edge

Achieve this by using **Refine Edge/Select** and **Mask** (more below)

Useful for seamless edits to faces, objects with complex edges, etc.

Hard edge:

Defines a precise, cut-out selection

Created with Marquee tools or Polygonal Lasso

Useful when you need defined selections for animations, composites, etc.

✓ **Adjusting Selection Edges**

Often your initial selection will need some refinement to accurately isolate your desired area. Here are some tips:

Refine Edge/Select and Mask - Access advanced selection controls like edge radius, decontaminate colors, etc.

Feather - Soften the hard edge by feathering/blurring the border

Contract/Expand - Shrink or enlarge the selection by a set number of pixels

Grow/Similar - Expand a selection to include similar colors based on the initial selection

Take time to refine your edges for professional results in your layered images, masks, and more.

Making Selections

✓ Rectangular Marquee Tool

The Rectangular Marquee allows you to select rectangular and square areas in an image.

To use:

Select the Rectangular Marquee in the Tools panel.

Drag to draw a rectangle over the desired area.

For a perfect square, hold Shift while dragging.

You can also click once in the image to create a rectangle of set size and proportions. Useful for selecting specific areas like 500x500 pixels.

✓ Elliptical Marquee Tool

The Elliptical Marquee selects oval and circular areas in an image.

To use:

Select the Elliptical Marquee in the Tools panel.

Drag to draw an oval over the desired area.

Hold Shift for a perfect circle.

Alt-click to draw the selection outwards from the center spot.

Quickly select subjects like faces, eyes, and more with the Elliptical Marquee.

✓ **Lasso Tool**

The Lasso allows you to make freeform selections by drawing loosely around an area.

To use:

Select the Lasso in the Tools panel.

Click and drag to trace the edge of the desired selection.

Release back at the starting point to complete the selection.

The Lasso is great for making organic, hand-drawn selections.

✓ Polygonal Lasso Tool

The Polygonal Lasso makes selections based on straight-line segments.

To use:

Select the Polygonal Lasso in the Tools panel.

Click to set the starting point, then click again to set each segment.

Double-click to complete the selection.

Alt-click to undo segments.

Use the Polygonal Lasso for man-made objects and hard-edged selections.

✓ Magnetic Lasso Tool

The Magnetic Lasso automatically snaps to edges as you draw around elements.

To use:

Select the Magnetic Lasso in the Tools panel.

Click to set the starting point on an edge.

Trace around the desired area. The selection will snap to detected edges.

Double-click to complete.

The Magnetic Lasso is perfect for quickly selecting objects and subjects against high-contrast backgrounds.

✓ **Quick Selection Tool**

The Quick Selection tool lets you paint over an area to automatically select it based on tone and color.

To use:

Select the Quick Selection in the Tools panel.

Drag to paint over the area you want to select. The selection will expand to include similar tones and colors.

Hold Alt to subtract from the selection.

Adjust tolerance in Options for more/less accuracy.

Quickly make complex selections with a few strokes using the Quick Selection tool.

✓ **Magic Wand Tool**

The Magic Wand allows you to select similarly colored regions in an image with one click.

To use:

Select the Magic Wand in the Tools panel.

Click on an area of solid color in the image.

The selection will expand to include contiguous pixels within the tolerance set in Options.

Adjust tolerance to fine-tune selected regions.

The Magic Wand is ideal for quickly selecting regions of solid color like skies, walls, etc.

✓ **Color Range Selection**

The Color Range command selects parts of an image based on a sample color.

To use:

Go to **Select > Color Range**.

Use the Eyedropper to choose a sample color from the image.

Fine-tune the selection using the Fuzziness and Range sliders.

Click OK to finalize the color-based selection.

Color Range is excellent for selections based on color such as blue skies, green screens, etc.

✓ Select Menu Commands

The Select menu contains useful commands for working with selections:

Select All: Instantly select the entire canvas.

Reselect: Quickly reselect your previous selection.

Inverse: Flips the selection to everything currently not selected.

Modify: Opens selection adjustment options like Border, Smooth, etc.

Master these handy Select menu commands to boost your workflow.

Refining Selections

Whether making complex selections or isolating subtle details, it's likely your initial selection will need some refinement.

✓ Adding to Selections

You'll often need to add or append to an existing selection to include more area. Here are two ways to do this:

Add with selection tools:

Make a new selection with any tool like the Lasso while holding Shift. This combines the new selection with your previous selection.

Select > Modify > Expand:

Expand your selection outward by the number of pixels you enter. Useful for growing a selection uniformly.

✓ Subtracting from Selections

Subtracting lets you carve away areas you don't want selected. Options include:

Subtract with selection tools:

Make a new selection with any tool while holding Alt. This subtracts the new selection from your current selection.

Select > Modify > Contract:

Contracts your selection inward by the number of pixels entered. Good for uniformly shrinking the selection.

✓ Inverting Selections

Inverting flips or reverses your selection so the unselected area becomes selected (and vice versa).

To invert:

Press Ctrl/Cmd + Shift + I

Or go to **Select > Inverse**

This is useful when you want to select everything except a particular area.

✓ **Feathering Selections**

Feathering blurs the border of a selection so the edge blends with the background.

To feather:

Make a selection and go to **Select > Modify > Feather**

Enter feather radius in pixels (1-250)

Higher values increase the feather amount.

Feathering produces smoother, more natural selections.

✓ **Smoothing Selections**

The Smooth option reduces irregularities or "hairy" boundaries in a selection.

To smooth:

Make a selection and go to **Select > Modify > Smooth**

Enter smooth radius in pixels (1-100).

Higher values increase the smoothness.

Smoothing polished jagged selections.

Refining selections may take some trial and error, but it's key for professional results. Start with your base selection, then add or subtract areas as needed.

Working with Selections

Making a selection is just the starting point. Once you've isolated an area, there are myriad ways to work with and manipulate selections to achieve your desired effect.

✓ Moving Selections

Once made, you can freely move selections to any area on the canvas:

Click inside the selection with the Move tool

Drag to move the selection outline to the desired location

The pixels will move with the selection border

Moving is useful for duplicating objects, arranging compositions, and more.

✓ Copying Selections

In addition to moving, you can copy selections:

Make a selection with any tool then hold Alt

Click inside the selection and drag to copy it

This pastes the selection + content onto a new area

Copying is great for duplicating elements and building up complex scenes.

✓ Deleting Selections

Deleting removes the selected area, leaving a transparent background behind:

Make a selection, then press Delete

The selection disappears, revealing transparency

Or use the Eraser tool to selectively erase just parts of a selection

Delete unwanted objects or create transparency with this technique.

✓ **Filling Selections**

You can fill selections with colors, patterns, or textures for interesting effects:

Make a selection, then go to **Edit > Fill**

Choose a Fill Type (color, gradient, pattern, etc.)

Click OK to fill the selection with your chosen fill

Get creative and fill selections in various ways.

✓ **Stroking Selections**

Stroking "paints" along the border of a selection:

Make a selection, choose a foreground color

Go to **Edit > Stroke**

Set Stroke Width in pixels

Click OK to outline the selection edges

Add colored borders and creative frames using the Stroke command.

✓ **Loading Selections**

Save a selection as a channel to reload it later:

Make a selection then go to **Select > Save Selection**

Name the selection channel

Later, choose **Load Selection** to reload the saved selection

Reuse selections without having to recreate them from scratch.

✓ **Saving Selections**

Take it a step further by saving selections as alpha channels:

Make a selection, go to **Select > Save Selection**

Choose **New Channel** from the dropdown

Give the channel a descriptive name

The selection is saved as an alpha channel in the Channels panel

Saving as an alpha makes the selection easily accessible from any document.

Masks

Masks selectively conceal and reveal parts of a layer or image. There are two types:

Layer masks: Hide/show areas on a layer using a greyscale mask image. Black conceals, white reveals.

Vector masks: Use shapes and paths to mask layers. Crisp, resolution-independent edges.

Masks enable non-destructive editing. You can modify masks as needed without damaging the source content.

✓ Using Layer Masks

Layer masks offer flexible selective editing:

Create a layer mask: Click the **Add Layer Mask** button in the **Layers** panel

Paint mask: Use Brush/Gradient tools to "paint" black/white on the mask

Density controls opacity: Shades of gray make partially transparent masks

Invert mask: Swap hidden/visible areas

Layer masks are perfect for soft, natural blending and adjustments.

Create from Selections:

Make a selection on a layer

Right-click and choose Layer Via Copy or Layer Via Cut

The selection will be copied/cut to a new masked layer

✓ **Using Vector Masks**

Vector masks use paths to define sharp-edged masked areas:

Create a vector mask: Click the Add Vector Mask button in the Layers panel

Define shape: Draw a path with the Pen or Shape tools

Path hides layer: The path defines mask edges based on transparency

Resize freely: Vector masks remain smooth at any size or resolution

Vector masks excel for graphic elements like text or logos.

✓ **Editing and Refining Masks**

Fine-tune masks in Quick Mask mode:

Enter Quick Mask mode: Click the **Quick Mask** button at the bottom of the **Layers** panel

Paint with black/white to hide/reveal on mask

Adjust opacity for soft edges

Exit Quick Mask to apply changes

Quick Mask gives you freehand control when masks need refinement.

CHAPTER FIVE

Bitmap Image Modes

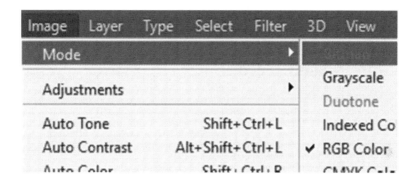

Bitmap images contain only two colors - black and white. They are distinct from raster images, which can contain millions of colors. Bitmap files require less storage space and can be easily resized without losing quality.

The three bitmap modes we'll cover are:

Bitmap: Pure black and white pixels. Best for simple icons and logos.

Grayscale: Shades of gray representing light and dark. Good for black and white photos.

Duotone: Black plus one additional color. Provides a bold, high-contrast effect.

Now let's look at how to convert an image and work in each mode.

✓ **Using Bitmap Mode**

Open your image in Photoshop 2024.

Go to **Image > Mode > Bitmap.**

In the Bitmap dialog box, choose a Resolution (higher is better).

For Method, choose Halftone Screen for photos or Diffusion Dither for graphics.

Click OK.

Once in Bitmap mode, you only have black and white pixels to work with. Use the Brush and Eraser tools to tidy up your image. The Paint Bucket tool fills areas with black or white.

Use Bitmap mode for things like website icons, logos, or silhouetted images. Just be aware that it doesn't handle nuance or gradients well.

✓ **Using Grayscale Mode**

Grayscale mode uses different shades of gray to represent an image, from white to black. Use it for any black-and-white imagery. Follow these steps:

Open your image and make sure it's flattened.

Go to **Image > Mode > Grayscale**.

Click Discard in the dialog box to convert to grayscale.

Now you can adjust the brightness and contrast to fine-tune your image. Use the Dodge and Burn tools to lighten or darken areas. The Brush tool paints in shades of gray.

Grayscale is ideal for old black-and-white photographs. The range of grays allows you to preserve detail. You can also convert color images to grayscale to create interesting high-contrast effects.

✓ Using Duotone Mode

Duotone mode lets you create a two-color version of a grayscale image. This uses black ink plus one other ink color, such as red, blue, gold, etc. To use duotone mode:

Convert your image to Grayscale first.

Go to **Image > Mode > Duotone**.

In the Duotone Options dialog, click the color box to choose your second color.

Click OK to convert to duotone.

In duotone mode, you can adjust the balance between the black and secondary color ink to change the mood and contrast of the image.

Duotones provide an eye-catching, high-contrast effect. They work best with photos containing bold shapes. Duotone images stand out beautifully when printed.

RGB Color Modes

RGB stands for the three primary colors used for displaying images on computers and mobile devices:

- ✓ Red
- ✓ Green
- ✓ Blue

By mixing varying intensities of these colors, RGB can reproduce millions of other colors. RGB color relies on light.

Working in RGB Color Mode

RGB is the best mode for on-screen design work. This includes:

✓ Websites

✓ Presentations

✓ Digital ads

✓ Video editing

✓ Mobile apps

✓ Anything intended for screens

To set a document to RGB mode:

Go to **Image > Mode > RGB Color**.

In the dialog box, click OK.

In RGB mode, you have access to millions of colors. Use adjustment layers to fine-tune hues and saturation. Save your finished design as a JPG or PNG to retain RGB colors.

✓ **Converting to CMYK Color Mode**

Use CMYK mode when preparing designs for professional printing. The CMYK inks reproduce a wide gamut of colors.

To convert to CMYK:

Go to **Image > Mode > CMYK Color**.

In the dialog box, click OK.

In CMYK mode, avoid using specialty colors not intended for print. Stick to solid CMYK colors only.

Photoshop warns you when opening a CMYK document since colors may shift slightly. Feel free to convert back to RGB for on-screen work at any time.

✓ **Using Lab Color Mode**

Lab Color is useful when you need precise control over color adjustments. To convert to Lab Color:

Go to **Image > Mode > Lab Color**.

Click OK in the dialog box.

In Lab mode, you can adjust the lightness channel separately from the green-to-red and blue-to-yellow color channels. Use Lab for color correction on photos.

✓ **Converting Between Color Modes**

Use these steps to convert between RGB, CMYK, and Lab Color modes:

Go to **Image > Mode.**

Select the color mode you want.

In the dialog box, click OK.

Photoshop will handle the conversion for you. Just be aware that some color shifts may occur when switching modes.

Understanding Color Depth

Color depth is determined by the number of bits used to represent the color of each pixel in an image. More bits mean more colors are available.

The three options in Photoshop 2024 are:

8-bit: 16.7 million colors

16-bit: 281 trillion colors

32-bit: 4.3 billion colors

A higher color depth reduces banding and increases editing flexibility. The best option depends on your specific image and workflow.

✓ Editing in 8-Bit Color

8-bit color uses 8 bits per channel, allowing for 256 possible shades per Red, Green, and Blue channel. This equates to roughly 16.7 million possible colors.

8-bit is the standard mode for most images. It offers a wide color range while keeping file sizes manageable. Uses include:

- ✓ Digital photography
- ✓ Web images like JPGs
- ✓ Illustrations and print projects

8-bit is also the default color depth for new Photoshop documents. Feel free to adjust levels, curves, hues, and saturation with all the colors available in 8-bit mode.

✓ Working in 16-Bit Color

16-bit color uses 16 bits per channel, resulting in over 281 trillion possible colors. This extensive color range reduces banding issues (sudden jumps between shades).

Uses for 16-bit color include:

- ✓ Professional photo editing
- ✓ Image manipulation with layers
- ✓ Preparing files for print

16-bit allows for more precise adjustments when editing photos. Transition gradients are smoother, with minimal quality loss between edits. The expanded range gives you greater creative freedom.

✓ Editing in 32-Bit Color

32-bit color uses 32 bits per channel, supporting over 4.3 billion colors per channel. This high bit depth makes gradients ultra smooth.

32-bit shines when:

- ✓ Combining images with layers

✓ Performing multiple edits and transformations

✓ Creating complex digital compositions

The massive color range prevents quality degradation across repeated edits. Use 32-bit to maintain pristine accuracy when compositing images. Just be aware of the large file sizes.

✓ **Converting Between Color Depths**

It's easy to switch between 8-bit, 16-bit, and 32-bit color in Photoshop:

Click **Image > Mode** in the menu bar.

Select the desired bit depth.

Click OK.

Photoshop will handle converting to your new color depth. Higher to lower bit depths may cause minor quality loss. But you can always go up again for non-destructive editing.

Color Management

Color management provides uniform color interpretation between input (cameras, scanners), displays, and output (printers, presses). It works by using color profiles that define the color space of devices.

Benefits of color management include:

✓ Accurate, consistent color rendering

✓ Colors match across editing sessions, programs, and devices

✓ Reduced guesswork and manual color corrections

Photoshop provides built-in color settings and tools to implement color management. Let's look at the key steps.

Assigning Color Profiles

Assigning the proper color profile ensures accurate color interpretation. Here's how:

✓ Open your image and confirm the correct RGB or CMYK color space.

✓ Go to **Edit > Assign Profile**.

✓ Choose the corresponding profile: Adobe RGB or sRGB for RGB images, or U.S. Web Coated (SWOP) v2 for CMYK images.

✓ Click OK.

✓ The color profile is now embedded in your image file for consistent coloring.

Working with Embedded and Missing Profiles

Some images you work with may already contain embedded color profiles, while others don't. Here's how to handle both cases:

✓ **Embedded Profiles**

If the embedded profile matches your workspace, you can leave it as is.

If the profiles differ, Photoshop will ask how to handle the mismatch. Choose Convert to Workspace to reconcile.

✓ **Missing Profiles**

For images without profiles, assign the appropriate RGB or CMYK profile as outlined above.

Avoid assigning mismatched profiles as this can shift colors incorrectly.

Adhering to color workflows avoids unpredictable color shifts when sharing files.

Converting Document Color Profiles

When you need to change an image's current color profile, use these steps:

Go to **Edit > Convert to Profile**.

Under Destination Space, select the new profile: sRGB for web, Adobe RGB for print, etc.

Click OK to convert.

Keep in mind that converting between some profiles can alter or reduce your color range. But this ensures your image follows the proper workflow.

Colors for Web

Unlike print design, web design must account for different browser interpretations of RGB colors.

Follow these Photoshop 2024 tips for managing your palette:

Use the indexed color mode with color tables for consistent results.

Stick to web-safe colors that display well across browsers.

Use hex codes for precision color selection.

Save and export files properly for the web and screens.

Let's look at each of these topics in more detail.

✓ Using Indexed Color Mode

Indexed color mode restricts your palette to 256 colors optimized for the web. To use it:

Go to **Image > Mode > Indexed Color**.

In the dialog box, choose the Web option and click OK.

This builds a color table best suited for the web. You can edit the table to customize your palette further.

Indexed color ensures your colors translate properly online without unpredictable shifts.

✓ **Working with Web-Safe Colors**

Web-safe colors are 216 specific RGB values known to render correctly in browsers. To view web-safe colors:

Open the Color Picker.

Click Only Web Colors.

This displays the standard web-safe palette for you to sample from. Or reference web-safe color codes when editing.

Stick to these colors for design elements like text and backgrounds to avoid inconsistencies.

✓ **Using Hexadecimal Color Codes**

Hex codes define colors with a 6-digit combination of letters A-F and numbers 0-9. For example, pure red is #FF0000.

Benefits of using hex codes include:

Precisely selection of colors.

Match colors used on website CSS.

Communicate color choices.

Have your developer provide webpage hex codes to match during design.

✓ **Saving and Exporting for Web**

Always save and export your web images properly:

Save web images in standard RGB mode.

Export assets as JPGs or PNGs with appropriate compression.

Ensure files are correctly sized for your website layout.

This produces optimized web graphics with indexed, web-safe colors.

CHAPTER SIX

Tone and Color Correction

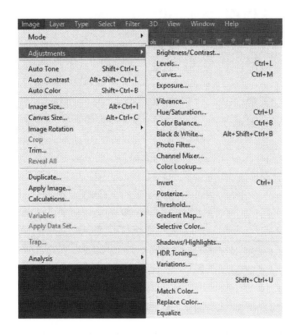

While there are many ways to make adjustments in Photoshop 2024, we'll look at some common effective tools for tone and color adjustments. With practice and experimentation, you'll be able to use these tools individually or in combination to correct any photo.

✓ **Brightness/Contrast**

The Brightness/Contrast adjustment is a quick and easy way to make basic changes to the tonal range of the image. This tool can correct underexposed or overexposed photos or create graphic high-contrast effects.

To use it:

Go to **Image > Adjustments > Brightness/Contrast**

Drag the sliders to adjust brightness up/down and contrast up/down.

Click okay when adjustments are complete.

Use brightness to lighten or darken the overall image. Contrast expands or reduces the difference between the darker and lighter areas.

✓ **Levels**

The Level adjustment gives you more precise control over the tonal range of an image. You can adjust the shadows, midtones, and highlights separately using the sliders.

To use Levels:

Go to **Image > Adjustments > Levels**

Drag the black slider to adjust the dark areas. Slide left to darken shadows or right to lighten them.

Drag the grey slider to adjust midtones. Slide left to darken or right to lighten.

Drag the white slider to adjust highlights. Slide left to reduce blown-out areas or right to brighten them.

Adjust the Output sliders to fine-tune brightness or contrast.

Click okay when adjustments are complete.

Take your time when moving the sliders to prevent clipping and blowing out your highlights and shadows. Levels give you amazing control over the tonal scale.

✓ **Curves**

The Curves adjustment tool provides precise tonal control using a visual graph interface. It allows you to manually adjust different points along the tonal range.

To use Curves:

Go to **Image > Adjustments > Curves**

Click and drag the curve line up or down at different points to adjust brightness.

Use the bottom left area for shadows, mid-curve for midtones, and upper right for highlights.

Click okay when adjustments are complete.

With practice, Curves allow for very nuanced brightness and contrast enhancements. Subtle changes can make a big difference.

✓ **Vibrance**

To adjust the intensity of colors without oversaturating an image, use the Vibrance tool. It will boost weaker colors more than already saturated colors.

To use Vibrance:

Go to **Image > Adjustments > Vibrance**

Drag the slider right to increase color vibrance or left to decrease it.

Click okay when finished.

Vibrance gives photos a nice boost in color while keeping skin tones looking natural. Overuse can cause an artificial neon effect.

✓ **Hue/Saturation**

For targeted color adjustments, use the Hue/Saturation tool. You can adjust all colors or select a specific color range to change.

To use Hue/Saturation:

Go to **Image > Adjustments > Hue/Saturation**

Drag the saturation slider right to increase or left to decrease overall color intensity.

Click the dropdown menu to choose a specific color range to adjust.

Drag the hue slider to shift colors clockwise or counter-clockwise.

Adjust lightness to brighten or darken the selected color range.

Click okay when finished.

This tool is handy for correcting color casts or shifting colors to be more natural or stylistic. Use it sparingly to avoid overdone effects.

✓ **Black & White**

To quickly convert a color image to black and white or greyscale, use the Black and white adjustment layer. You can precisely control how each color converts to a shade of grey.

To use Black & White:

Go to **Image > Adjustments > Black & White**

Adjust the color sliders to control how each color converts from color to greyscale. For example, boosting yellows will brighten them.

Click okay when the contrast looks good.

For more control, use Black and white as an adjustment layer instead of a standard adjustment. This allows you to tweak the effect or erase it from parts of the image.

Image Enhancement

Image enhancement improves the aesthetic appearance of a photo. This involves processing techniques that alter pixels to adjust brightness, shadows, sharpness, noise, and other elements. When done right, enhancement draws viewers into an image and creates more depth and vibrance.

✓ **Shadows/Highlights**

The Shadows/Highlights tool lets you brighten shadows and darken highlights to reveal hidden details. This can rescue photos with contrast issues.

To use Shadows/Highlights:

Go to **Image > Adjustments > Shadows/Highlights**

Drag the Shadows slider right to lighten dark areas.

Drag the Highlights slider left to darken bright areas.

Adjust the Midtone slider to fine-tune the contrast.

Click okay when details are revealed.

Use this tool sparingly as it can cause noise and a halo effect if overused. It's perfect for lifting shadows to uncover details.

✓ **HDR Toning**

HDR Toning blends multiple exposure levels to create stunning contrast and color effects. These mimics the look of a High Dynamic Range photo.

To use HDR Toning:

Go to **Image> Adjustments > HDR Toning**

Check the Preview box to see the initial effect.

Adjust the Toning sliders to customize the look.

Click okay to apply the HDR style to your photo.

HDR Toning works best on images with a wide tonal range. Use it sparingly to avoid an overdone surreal effect.

Creative Color Effects

Color effects allow you to stylize and enhance photos beyond basic corrections. They can turn mundane pictures into eye-catching works of art. From bold gradients to retro pixelation, the options are endless.

✓ Posterize

The Posterize tool reduces the number of color levels in a photo to make it look hand-painted or graphic. You control the level of posterization.

To use Posterize:

Go to **Image > Adjustments > Posterize**

Lower the levels slider to reduce color gradations.

Click OK when you achieve the desired comic or pop art look.

Try layers to limit posterizing to certain elements, like the background. This effect works great on high-contrast photos.

✓ **Threshold**

Threshold converts color images to stark black and white using a set brightness threshold. This bold graphic look isolates shapes and contours.

To use Threshold:

Go to **Image > Adjustments >Threshold**

Adjust the level slider to increase or decrease the threshold.

Click OK when you achieve the desired silhouette effect.

Use layers to keep some elements in color for extra impact. Threshold works well on images with defined shapes and outlines.

✓ **Gradient Map**

The Gradient Map effect maps image tones to a gradient fill for bold colorful renders. The gradient colors replace the original hues.

To use Gradient Map:

Go to **Image > Adjustments > Gradient Map**

Click the gradient bar to open the Gradient Editor.

Select a preset gradient or create a custom one.

Click OK to apply the gradient colors to your photo.

Try combining Gradient Map with Blend Modes like Overlay to mix the effect with the original colors. Vivid gradients lend an intense, fantasy feel.

✓ **Selective Color**

Selective color isolates and transforms a single color range while keeping the rest of the photo black and white. This draws attention to key elements.

To use Selective Color:

Go to **Image > Adjustments > Selective Color**

Click the color range dropdown and select the color to isolate.

Adjust the sliders to transform the selected color.

Click OK when you achieve the desired emphasis effect.

Use careful selections to isolate specific colored elements. Try shifting reds to purple or yellows to orange. Selective color is an easy way to make colors pop.

Applying Adjustments

Photoshop adjustments can improve contrast, correct color casts, add creative effects, and much more. But directly applying adjustments permanently alters pixel values, limiting flexibility. Adjustment layers solve this by applying non-destructive edits you can tweak or remove.

Adjustment Layers

Adjustment layers apply enhancements without permanently changing pixels. You can modify or delete the adjustments later.

To use adjustment layers:

- ✓ Open the image to enhance.
- ✓ Click the **Adjustment Layer** icon at the bottom of the Layers panel.
- ✓ Choose an adjustment like **Levels, Curves,** or **Color Balance**.
- ✓ Tweak settings in the **Properties** panel.
- ✓ Use layer masks to limit the adjustment to certain areas.

Benefits include re-editing anytime and stacking multiple adjustment layers to combine effects.

Fill Layers

Fill layers and add gradient or pattern overlays to images non-destructively. This provides creative effects and textures.

To use fill layers:

- ✓ Click the **Create New Fill** or **Adjustment Layer** icon at the bottom of the **Layers** panel.
- ✓ Choose either **Gradient** or **Pattern**.
- ✓ Customize the gradient or pattern settings.

✓ Change the layer blend mode to modify the effect.

✓ Add layer masks to limit the fill to only certain parts of the image.

Get creative with fill layers to add depth, focal points, or interest to boring backgrounds.

Blending Modes

Blending modes control how the pixel values of adjustment layers mix with the layers below them. This creates cool creative effects.

To use blending modes:

✓ Apply an adjustment layer to your image.

✓ In the Layers panel, change the blending mode of the adjustment layer.

✓ Try different modes like Screen, Multiply, Overlay, Soft Light, Hard Light, etc.

✓ Lower the Opacity of the layer to fine-tune the effect intensity.

Blending modes are useful for creating unique stylized versions of photos. Experiment with different modes and opacity levels.

CHAPTER SEVEN

Adding Text

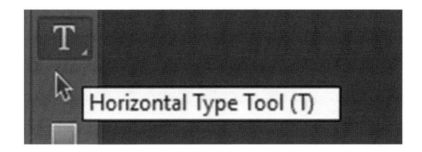

The Type Tool is located in the Tools panel, which is docked on the left side of the Photoshop workspace. You can also select it quickly by pressing the letter **T** on your keyboard.

To add text with the Type Tool:

Select the Type Tool in the Tools panel.

Choose a font family, font style, font size, alignment, and color in the Options Bar at the top of the screen. This will set the default look of your text.

Click anywhere in your document to add a text layer and start typing. A new layer called **"Type"** will appear in the Layers panel.

Now you know how to activate the Type Tool and begin adding text. Next, let's cover the different types of text you can create.

Typing Text

With the Type Tool selected, you can click and type text anywhere in your Photoshop document. Where and how you click will determine whether you create point or paragraph text.

Creating Point Text

✓ To create point text, simply click once with the Type Tool and then start typing. This will add a single line of horizontal text at the point where you clicked.

✓ Point text is useful for short phrases, labels, logos, headlines, or any other small text elements.

✓ To finish entering point text, click the check mark in the Options Bar or press Enter on your keyboard.

Creating Paragraph Text

✓ To create paragraph text, click and drag with the Type Tool to draw out a text box, then start typing within the box. The text will wrap to fill the box.

✓ Use paragraph text whenever you need multiple lines of text, like body copy, descriptions, or blocks of text.

✓ To finish entering paragraph text, click outside of the text box or press Ctrl + Enter or Cmd + Enter on your keyboard.

Creating Path Text

In addition to straight point and paragraph text, you can make text flow along a custom path or shape. This is called path text or type on a path.

To create text on a path:

✓ Draw and position the path you want using the Pen or Shape tools.

✓ Select the Type Tool and hover over the path until the cursor changes to an I-beam with a curved line under it.

✓ Click once on the path and start typing. The text will automatically follow the line of the path.

✓ When you are done, click the check mark in the Options Bar.

Using text on a path is great for adding text to circles, making text flow around shapes, or adding artistic typography styles.

Formatting Text

Text formatting gives you precise control over the appearance and layout of text. Proper formatting enhances readability and makes text more visually engaging.

Changing Font Family and Style

One of the fastest ways to update the look of text is to change the font. Photoshop gives you access to thousands of fonts that you can use in your documents.

To change the font family and style:

- ✓ Select the Type Tool and click on the text layer you want to edit.
- ✓ Look at the font family and font style options in the Options Bar across the top of the screen.
- ✓ Click the drop-down menus to select a new font family and font style. For example, you can select "Bold" or "Italic" as the font style.
- ✓ You can also access advanced font filters and preview options by clicking on the filters icon in the font family drop-down.

Adjusting Font Size

In addition to changing the font itself, you can also adjust the size of the text. Use larger sizes for titles and headings, and smaller sizes for body text.

To change the font size:

- ✓ Select your text with the **Type Tool**.

✓ In the **Options Bar**, enter the desired font size in the size field. You can enter any number, or use the up and down arrows to adjust the size.

✓ You can also change sizes incrementally by using keyboard shortcuts. Press **Cmd/Ctrl + Shift + >** to increase or **Cmd/Ctrl + Shift + <** to decrease size.

✓ Font size will depend on how the text will be used and the overall layout of your design. Ensure the body text is large enough to read easily.

Leading/Line Spacing

Leading (pronounced "ledding") refers to the vertical space between lines of text, also known as line spacing. Adjusting leading helps control the readability and density of text.

To change leading:

✓ Select the text you want to adjust.

✓ Go to the Character panel and look for the Leading option.

✓ Increase or decrease the number to control the space between lines of text.

✓ Generally, the leading should be set between 120% - 150% of the font size for optimum readability. However, creative designs sometimes use tighter or looser leading.

Kerning and Tracking

Kerning and tracking allow you to control the spacing and proportion between letters and words. This significantly improves readability.

Kerning adjusts the space between individual letters while tracking adjusts spacing uniformly over a text selection.

To kern text:

✓ Select the Type Tool and click between the two letters you want to kern.

✓ In the Character panel menu, change the kerning values to move letters closer together or farther apart.

To track text:

- ✓ Highlight the text you want to track.
- ✓ In the Character panel menu, enter positive or negative tracking values to increase or decrease spacing.
- ✓ Use kerning and tracking sparingly to maintain legibility. Too much adjustment can distort the text.

Text Alignment

Alignment controls how text is positioned horizontally across a text box or line. Photoshop offers several text alignment options.

To set text alignment:

Select the paragraph text you want to align.

Click one of the alignment icons in the Options Bar:

Left aligned: Text is aligned evenly with a left edge but ragged on the right edge.

Centered: Text is centered within the text area.

Right aligned: Text is aligned evenly with a right edge but ragged on the left edge.

Justified: Text is aligned evenly along both the left and right edges.

Choose the type of alignment that works best for your design goals and layout.

Color and Style

Applying color and text style transforms basic text into eye-catching typographic elements. Use color to complement a design or make text stand out. Text styles like italics or 'underline' can also help convey meaning.

To quickly format text:

- ✓ Select the Type Tool and highlight your text.
- ✓ Open the Character panel to access controls for color and style.
- ✓ Click the color swatch to open the color picker and change the text color.
- ✓ Check boxes for Bold, Italic, All Caps, Underline, Strikethrough, etc.

Take formatting even further by applying Layer Styles for effects like shadows, glows, and more.

Text Layers

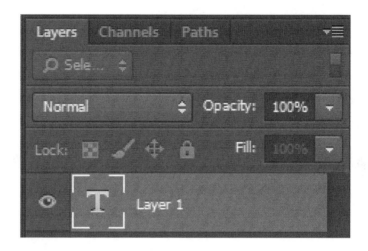

When you add text with the Type Tool, Photoshop automatically places the text on its layer. The layer is named "T" by default.

Working with text on layers rather than directly on your image gives you more flexibility. You can easily move, edit, or apply effects to text without permanently altering underlying image layers.

Convert to Shape

You can convert editable text into a vector shape. This changes the text from a text layer into a shape layer, so you can no longer edit the words directly. But shapes give you different creative options.

To convert text to shape:

- ✓ Select the Type Tool and click the text layer to edit.
- ✓ Right-click the text layer and choose **"Convert to Shape."**
- ✓ The text will shift from a text layer to a vector shape layer.
- ✓ Now you can resize, distort, or apply effects to the text shape!

Rasterize Type

Rasterizing converts text into a flat image on a regular pixel layer. This baked-in version of the text is no longer resizable or editable.

Rasterize type when you want to apply filters or effects that aren't compatible with vector text layers.

To rasterize text:

- ✓ Select the text layer.
- ✓ Right-click the layer and choose **"Rasterize Type."**
- ✓ The text will become an uneditable image layer.
- ✓ Use rasterized text when you need a specific effect like a glass texture or glow.

Type Masks

A type mask uses text to mask out underlying layers, revealing the background. The text becomes a vector mask that shows through to whatever is behind it.

To create a type mask:

- ✓ Add a text layer on top of an image layer.
- ✓ In the Layers panel, right-click the text layer and select **"Create Clipping Mask."**

✓ The text will cut its shape out of the image below it.

✓ Adjust the text to change what part of the image shows through.

Vector Masks

You can also use any vector shape as a text mask. Just like a text-clipping mask, the shape will cut its outline out of the text.

To use a shape to mask text:

Add a text layer and vector shape layer. Put the shape above the text.

Right-click the shape layer and choose **"Create Clipping Mask."**

The text will only be visible where the shape overlaps it.

Stroke Text

Adding a stroke applies color and thickness to the outline of text characters. This adds emphasis and makes the text stand out.

To add a text stroke:

- ✓ Double-click the text layer to edit the options.
- ✓ In the **Layer Style** panel, click Stroke.
- ✓ Adjust stroke color, size, position, and blend mode.
- ✓ Click OK to apply the stroke.
- ✓ Use strokes strategically to make key text elements pop.

Warp Text

The Warp Text options let you distort and bend text into fun shapes and effects. You can curve text, pinch it, inflate it, twist it, and more!

To warp text:

- ✓ Select the Type Tool and your text layer.
- ✓ Open the **Warp Text** menu in the top Options Bar.
- ✓ Pick a warp style like Arc or Bulge and adjust the sliders.
- ✓ Click the Warp button to apply the effect.

✓ Warp text when you want to incorporate typography into designs in artistic ways.

Paragraph Text Box

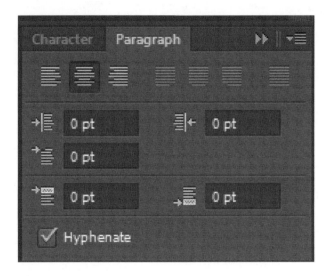

Paragraph text boxes are containers that hold multiple lines of text, also called body copy. Unlike point text, paragraph text automatically wraps within the boundaries you define.

Creating Paragraph Text Boxes

Adding paragraph text is easy with the Type Tool:

✓ Select the **Type Tool** in the Tools panel.

- ✓ Choose font, size, and other text options in the **Options Bar.**
- ✓ Click and drag on your document to draw out a text box.
- ✓ Start typing. Text will flow and wrap inside the box.
- ✓ Click outside the box when finished typing.
- ✓ Drawing a text box first before typing gives you a defined space for text to populate.

Resizing and Reflowing Paragraph Text

One advantage of paragraph text boxes is that you can quickly resize or change the shape of the box without having to reformat the text. As you resize the box, the text will automatically reflow to fit.

To resize an existing text box:

- ✓ Click inside the box with the Type Tool.
- ✓ Drag the round handles on the box edges to expand or contract the shape.
- ✓ Text will reflow dynamically as you resize. Expand to add more text, or shrink to limit text.

✓ Use the handles on the corners to proportionally scale the box.

✓ Resizing this way avoids messing up your text formatting.

Flowing Text Between Paragraph Boxes

You can link paragraph text boxes so text flows from one to the next as needed. This is useful for text that is longer than one box allows.

To flow text between boxes:

✓ Create two or more text boxes. Position them close together.

✓ Click inside the first box. Go to **Type > Paragraph**.

✓ Under Indents and Spacing, check the box for **"Text Flows Between Text Boxes."**

✓ Excess text from the first box will now flow into the next boxes.

✓ Linking text boxes gives you more flexibility for body copy.

Formatting Paragraph Text

Take advantage of Photoshop's text formatting options to style paragraph text:

- ✓ Set alignment, leading, tracking, etc. in the **Character** panel
- ✓ Use paragraph spacing and indent controls
- ✓ Add color, formatting, layer styles
- ✓ Rotate or transform text boxes
- ✓ Adjust blend mode and opacity of text box layers
- ✓ Combined with a defined text box, formatting makes polished paragraphs and columns of text.

Tips for Working with Paragraph Text

Keep these tips in mind for the best results:

- ✓ Draw an initial text box close to the final size needed to minimize reflowing

- ✓ Be precise when positioning multiple linked text boxes
- ✓ Adjust text box corners individually for angled or trapezoid shapes
- ✓ Use box transforms and rotations to create diagonals and curves
- ✓ Add a background color to make the text more readable
- ✓ With practice, you'll be able to create flowing text designs.

Text Effects

Text effects take typography beyond plain fonts. Using Photoshop 2024's array of effects tools, you can make text:

- ✓ Look three-dimensional with shadows and depth
- ✓ Simulate materials like metal, water, or fire
- ✓ Follow contours and shapes with warps
- ✓ Glow, fade, smear, blend, and much more.

Warp Effects

Photoshop's Warp Text tool lets you mold, bend, curve, and twist text into interesting shapes. Using it creates the illusion of distorted and morphed text.

To apply Warp effects:

- ✓ Create a type layer.
- ✓ Go to the Options Bar and select Warp Text.
- ✓ Pick a warp style like Arc or Inflate. Adjust the sliders.
- ✓ Click Warp to apply the distortion.

Drop Shadows

Adding a drop shadow to text simulates a light source cast on the letters, making them look more three-dimensional and prominent.

To give the text a drop shadow:

- ✓ Double-click the type layer to open Layer Style options.
- ✓ Select Drop Shadow and change the blend mode, color, distance, and other settings.

✓ Click OK to apply the shadow.

✓ Customize the angle, spread, and opacity of the shadow to get just the right effect.

Layer Styles

Photoshop includes many layer-style presets that add instant texturing, lighting, and dimension. Glows, bevels, and strokes are just a few effects available.

To use layer styles:

✓ Double-click the text layer.

✓ Select a style like Inner Shadow, Outer Glow, or Stroke.

✓ Adjust options like color, size, blend mode, and contour.

✓ Click OK to apply.

✓ Stack multiple-layer styles for unique combinations.

Blending Options

The Blending Options menu contains advanced controls for shadows, glows, overlays, textures, and more. Use these to create complex text effects.

To access Blending Options:

- ✓ Double-click the text layer.
- ✓ At the bottom of the Layer Style panel, click Blending Options.
- ✓ Adjust settings for glows, shadows, color overlays, textures, and strokes.
- ✓ Click OK to apply.

Tips for Text Effects

- ✓ Use subtle effects as accents instead of overdoing it.
- ✓ Adjust opacity and fill to create transparent effects.
- ✓ Align effects to the shape of text with layer style contours.
- ✓ Put text on its layer before applying effects.

- ✓ Try different blend modes like Multiply and Overlay.
- ✓ Add multiple layer styles and Blending Options for unique combinations.

Editing Text

One of the most common text edits is changing font properties like family, style, size, and formatting.

To edit font properties:

- ✓ Click the text layer with the Type tool to edit.
- ✓ Open the Options Bar. Change font, style, size, color, and alignment options.
- ✓ Use the buttons for Bold, Italic, Underline, and other styles.
- ✓ Right-click the layer to rasterize text if needed.
- ✓ Don't be afraid to experiment with different fonts and formatting.

Checking Spelling

Photoshop has a built-in spell-check feature to fix typos right within the app.

To check spelling:

- ✓ Click **Layer > Type > Check Spelling**.
- ✓ As Photoshop checks, misspellings will be highlighted.
- ✓ Right-click highlighted words to see suggestions and corrections.
- ✓ Choose Ignore or Change once you've fixed the typo.
- ✓ Run a spelling check as the final step before exporting your work.

Find and Replace

Searching for specific words or phrases to replace across your document is easy with Find and Replace.

To find and replace text:

- ✓ Go to **Edit > Find and Replace.**

✓ Enter the word or phrase to find in the **"Find"** field.

✓ Type the new text in the **"Replace"** field.

✓ Click **Replace** or **Replace All** to make the changes.

✓ This is much faster than manually searching.

Converting Text

For more editing flexibility, convert text to different formats like paragraph text, shapes, or rasterized pixels.

To convert text:

✓ Right-click a text layer and choose Convert to Paragraph Text or Convert to Shape.

✓ Rasterize the layer to convert it to pixels for applying filters.

✓ Converted text unlocks new creative options while retaining editability.

Tips for Editing Text

- ✓ Use keyboard shortcuts for font size (Cmd/Ctrl + Shift + > or <) and toggling styles like bold and italic.
- ✓ Adjust line spacing, kerning, and tracking for readability.
- ✓ Click and drag to select specific words or characters to edit.
- ✓ Set up paragraph styles for reusable formatting.
- ✓ Use the Move tool to reposition text boxes or lines.

CHAPTER EIGHT

Drawing Tools

Adobe Photoshop offers a robust set of drawing and painting tools that allow you to add creative flair and custom illustrations to your designs.

Pen Tool

The Pen tool allows you to draw smooth, precise vector paths and shapes. It works by placing anchor points as you click and controlling the curves between those points. Here's how to use it:

✓ Select the **Pen tool** from the Tools panel. It looks like a fountain pen icon.

✓ Click on your canvas to place an anchor point. Continue clicking to set additional points.

✓ To create curves, click and drag the mouse between two points. The longer the drag, the more dramatic the curve.

✓ Complete the path by clicking the initial anchor point.

✓ Adjust the path shape by clicking to select it, then adjusting the direction lines on the anchor points.

✓ Once finished, right-click and select a fill option like Shape or Path to convert the path into an editable shape or line.

Freeform Pen Tool

The Freeform Pen tool lets you draw freehand lines as if you were sketching with a pen or pencil. Follow these steps:

- ✓ Select the Freeform Pen tool from the Tools panel.
- ✓ Drag your mouse on the canvas to draw a freehand path.
- ✓ Release the mouse when you're finished drawing a stroke.
- ✓ Adjust line thickness by changing the Size setting in the options bar.
- ✓ Set options like pressure sensitivity to vary the stroke for natural effects.

✓ Complete the path or shape by clicking the initial start point.

Brush Tool

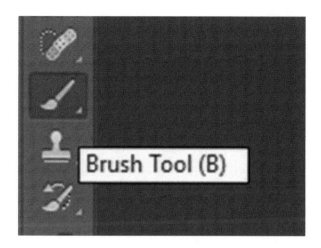

The Brush tool is useful for painting and drawing with organic, textured strokes. Here are some tips for using it:

✓ Choose a soft or hard-edged brush from the Brush Preset picker in the options bar.

✓ Adjust Size, Hardness, and other settings to customize your brush.

✓ Click and drag your mouse to paint or draw strokes.

✓ Use pressure sensitivity to vary stroke thickness.

✓ Select different blend modes and lower Opacity for transparent effects.

✓ Use the Mixer Brush to mix and blend paint colors on the canvas.

Pencil Tool

The Pencil tool creates hard-edged, freehand lines with a traditional pencil effect:

✓ Select the Pencil tool. Adjust Size and Hardness settings.

✓ Draw strokes by clicking and dragging your mouse.

✓ For shading effects, adjust the Opacity and Flow settings while dragging.

✓ Use pressure sensitivity for thickness variance.

✓ Right-click and select Fill Path to convert a closed path into a filled shape.

Mixer Brush Tool

The Mixer Brush simulates realistic painting by mixing colors on the canvas:

✓ Select the Mixer Brush and pick a brush from the Brush Preset picker.

✓ Adjust the Wet settings to control how much paint the brush picks up.

✓ Drag strokes across the canvas to mix and blend colors.

✓ Clean the brush periodically by holding Alt as you drag.

✓ Increase the Load setting to pick up more paint as you mix colors.

✓ Adjust how Wet the canvas is to make blending easier.

Eraser Tool

The Eraser tool removes areas of your drawing, similar to using an eraser on paper:

✓ Select the Eraser tool. Pick a soft or hard eraser from the Eraser Presets.

✓ Adjust Size, Opacity, and other settings to control the erased areas.

✓ Click and drag across your artwork to erase parts of your drawing.

✓ Use a soft-edged eraser at lower opacity for subtle shading effects.

✓ Change to Block mode to erase rectangular sections for cleaner results.

✓ Enable Erase to History to clear strokes down to the transparent canvas.

Shapes

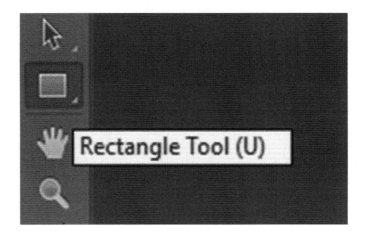

Photoshop 2024 provides a variety of shape tools that allow you to add simple or complex vector graphics to your designs. You can create standard shapes like rectangles and circles, custom shapes, and editable paths.

Rectangle Tool

The Rectangle tool creates rectangular and square vector shapes with customizable dimensions.

- ✓ Select the Rectangle tool from the Tools panel.
- ✓ On the options bar, enter measurements for Width and Height.
- ✓ Click and drag on the canvas to draw the shape. Hold Shift as you drag to draw a perfect square.
- ✓ Adjust dimensions at any time by selecting the shape and changing the Width and Height values.

Rounded Rectangle Tool

The Rounded Rectangle tool works the same as the Rectangle tool but adds adjustable corner roundness.

- ✓ Click and hold the Rectangle tool icon to select the Rounded Rectangle.

✓ Enter Width, Height, and Radius values on the options bar.

✓ Click and drag to draw a rectangle with rounded corners.

✓ Adjust the curve of the corners later by changing the Radius.

Ellipse Tool

The Ellipse tool lets you create circular, elliptical, and oval shapes.

✓ Click and hold the Rectangle tool icon to select the Ellipse.

✓ Enter Width and Height values for the ellipse dimensions.

✓ To draw a perfect circle, hold Shift while dragging.

✓ Click and drag to draw an elliptical shape on the canvas.

Polygon Tool

The Polygon tool makes it easy to draw triangles, hexagons, pentagons, and other multi-sided shapes.

- ✓ Select the Polygon tool and enter Sides and Radius values.
- ✓ Click and drag to draw the polygon shape.
- ✓ Adjust the appearance by changing the Radius or number of Sides.
- ✓ Select a polygon and right-click to choose a different Render option.

Line Tool

Use the Line tool to create straight-line paths and arrow shapes.

- ✓ Click and hold the Rectangle tool icon to select the Line tool.
- ✓ Enter a Length for the line and choose an arrowhead type.
- ✓ Click and drag to draw a straight line path on the canvas.

✓ Adjust length or arrowhead size by double-clicking the line shape.

Custom Shape Tool

✓ The Custom Shape tool lets you draw from preset vector shape packs and libraries.

✓ Select the Custom Shape tool. Pick a shape pack from the Shape picker.

✓ Click on the canvas to draw that custom shape.

✓ Right-click the shape layer to choose a different Fill color or Stroke.

✓ Load additional shape packs by clicking the gear icon in the Shape picker.

Paths

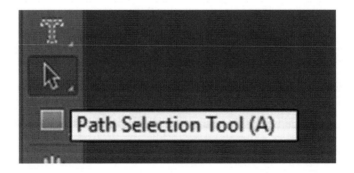

Paths allow you to create customizable vector shapes, lines, and curves. Unlike raster pixels, paths are vector-based, which means they can be scaled to any size without losing quality. Paths make it easy to design reusable elements like logos, icons, text effects, and more.

Creating Paths

You can make new paths using the Pen or Shape tools. Here's how:

- ✓ Select the **Pen tool**. Click anchor points to trace a path.
- ✓ For curves, click and drag to create direction lines.
- ✓ Complete the path by clicking the initial anchor point.
- ✓ To make a shape path, select the Shape tool. Choose an Ellipse, Polygon, etc.
- ✓ Click and drag on the canvas to trace a vector shape path.

Selecting Paths

To edit a path, you need to select it first:

- ✓ Click the Path Selection tool (black arrow) in the Tools panel.
- ✓ Click directly on an existing path to select the entire path.
- ✓ Drag a selection marquee around any portion of a path to select part of it.
- ✓ Press Ctrl/Cmd and click to add multiple paths to the selection.

Stroking Paths

Stroking outlines the path with color, like tracing it with a pen:

- ✓ Select the path with the Path Selection tool.
- ✓ Open the Stroke options in the options bar.
- ✓ Pick a color, thickness, and position for the stroke.
- ✓ Click Stroke in the options bar to outline the path.

Filling Paths

Filling adds color inside an enclosed path, like pouring paint inside:

- ✓ Select a closed path with the Path Selection tool.
- ✓ Open the Fill Path options in the options bar.
- ✓ Choose a fill color and mode like Normal or Gradient.
- ✓ Click Fill Path to fill the selection with color.

Loading Paths

You can load reusable custom path shapes using these steps:

- ✓ Select Load Paths from the Paths panel flyout menu.
- ✓ Browse and select a path file (.pth) containing your custom paths.
- ✓ Click the Load button to add the path shapes to your current document.
- ✓ Select a loaded path with the Path Selection tool to add it to your design.

Strokes

Strokes can add customizable outlines, borders, and embellishments to vector shapes, text, and selections. You have options to set stroke color, thickness, opacity, and more.

Solid Color Strokes

A solid color stroke outlines a shape or text with a uniform hue. Follow these steps:

- ✓ Select the shape layer or text to stroke.
- ✓ Open the Stroke options in the Properties panel.
- ✓ Choose a stroke color by clicking the color picker.
- ✓ Set stroke thickness in pixels.
- ✓ Click OK to apply the solid color outline.
- ✓ Adjust opacity to create transparent strokes.

Gradient Strokes

Gradient strokes fill the stroke area with a gradient blend of colors.

- ✓ Select the shape and open the Stroke options.
- ✓ Click the gradient bar to edit the gradient colors and style.
- ✓ Drag color stops to adjust the gradient blend.
- ✓ Set additional options like thickness and opacity.
- ✓ Click OK to stroke the shape with the gradient.

Pattern Strokes

For a textured stroke, use a repeating pattern:

- ✓ Open the Stroke options and click the pattern preset picker.
- ✓ Scroll through the patterns and select one to preview it.
- ✓ Adjust the scale to resize the pattern if needed.
- ✓ Click OK to stroke the selected area with the pattern.

✓ Lower opacity for a subtle pattern stroke.

✓ Click the gear icon in the pattern picker to load additional pattern libraries.

Shape Layers

Shape layers allow you to add and manipulate vector shapes like rectangles, ellipses, and custom paths. Unlike pixel layers, shape layers don't lose quality when resized. This makes them perfect for logos, icons, geometric patterns, and other resolution-independent graphics.

Vector Shape Layers

Shape layers have key advantages over plain pixel layers:

Scalable: Shape layers can be resized without quality loss.

Editable: Properties like color, effects, and fills can be edited.

Combinable: You can merge, subtract, and intersect shape layers.

Animatable: Shape paths and properties can be keyframed and animated.

To add a shape layer:

- ✓ Select a shape tool like Rectangle or Custom Shape.
- ✓ Draw a shape on the canvas by clicking and dragging.
- ✓ Right-click the shape layer to change the color, style, etc.

Transforming Shapes

You can easily transform shapes with no quality loss:

- ✓ Resize by dragging the side and corner handles.
- ✓ Rotate using the rotate handle or Free Transform.
- ✓ Flip shapes horizontally or vertically.
- ✓ Skew or distort using perspective handles.
- ✓ Adjust opacity and blend modes.

Boolean Operations

Combine shapes using Boolean operations:

Union: Merge two shapes.

Subtract Front Shape: Cut the top shape from the bottom shape.

Intersect: Keep just the overlapping area.

Exclude: Keep non-overlapping areas of shapes.

To use them, select two layers and choose an operation from the options bar.

Vector Masks

Vector masks allow you to precisely mask out portions of a layer using resolution-independent shapes and paths. The masked areas become transparent, revealing the layers below. Vector masks bring more flexibility and efficiency to complex masking tasks like silhouetting graphic elements and text.

Creating Vector Masks

Follow these steps to add a vector mask to a layer:

- ✓ Select the layer you want to mask.
- ✓ Click the **Add Vector Mask** button at the bottom of the **Layers** panel.
- ✓ Draw a path or shape over the areas to mask out using the vector tools.
- ✓ Adjust the path points and curves to refine the mask.
- ✓ Areas outside the path will be masked and become transparent.

Editing Vector Masks

You can edit a vector mask just like any path:

- ✓ Use the Direct Selection tool to adjust points and curve handles.
- ✓ Click the vector mask thumbnail to work directly on the mask path.
- ✓ Adjust overall mask feathering and density.
- ✓ Load or paste path shapes to add to the vector mask.

✓ Use Boolean operations to combine or subtract from the mask path.

Disabling Vector Masks

To turn off a vector mask temporarily:

✓ Click the **Disable/Enable** vector mask icon in the Layers panel.

✓ Shift-click the vector mask thumbnail to toggle it on and off.

✓ With the mask disabled, the full layer will be visible.

✓ Enable the mask again to hide the masked areas.

CHAPTER NINE

Painting Tools

Even if you're new to digital art or looking to touch up your painting skills, this topic will walk you through the basics of Photoshop 2024's painting toolset.

Brush Tool

The Brush Tool is likely the most commonly used painting tool in Photoshop. It allows you to paint smooth strokes of color onto your canvas. Here's how to use it:

✓ Select the **Brush Tool** from the toolbar. It's the icon that looks like a brush.

✓ In the top menu, choose a brush type. The brush presets menu has different brush tips like round, square, or scattered. Select one to fit your desired style.

✓ Adjust the brush size using the slider. Bigger sizes create bolder strokes.

✓ Set the hardness. A soft brush (low hardness) will have soft edges that blend. A hard brush (high hardness) has defined edges.

✓ Choose an opacity and flow. Lower opacity and flow values result in transparent and lighter strokes. Higher values make them more opaque and saturated.

✓ Pick a foreground color to paint with from the color picker.

✓ Start painting. Drag your mouse or use a graphics tablet stylus to create strokes. Use layers to ease editing.

Pencil Tool

The Pencil Tool lets you draw outlines and sketches in hard-edged pencil strokes. Here's how to use it:

- ✓ Select the Pencil Tool from the toolbar. It looks like a pencil icon.
- ✓ Adjust the pencil width using the slider. Thicker strokes are great for rough sketches. Thinner ones work for details and precision.
- ✓ Set the hardness. A soft pencil (low hardness) will make smoother lines that fade at the edges. A hard pencil (high hardness) draws sharp, defined lines.
- ✓ Lower the opacity for transparent, overlapping sketches. Higher opacity makes solid, opaque lines.
- ✓ Pick a foreground color. You can shade with gray tones or use vivid colors.
- ✓ Draw straight lines by click-dragging. For curves, click anchor points and drag the handles.

✓ Use layers to keep your sketchwork separate from other paintings.

The Pencil Tool excels at line art, comics, architectural sketches, and other drafts. Use it to plan out compositions before painting.

Color Replacement Tool

The Color Replacement Tool lets you quickly recolor areas of your artwork by painting over them. Follow these steps:

✓ Select the Color Replacement Tool from the toolbar. It has an icon of a scrub brush.

✓ Pick a foreground color from the color picker to replace existing colors.

✓ Drag your mouse or stylus over an area to replace its color with the foreground color.

✓ Adjust the tolerance to control how closely the replaced color must match your foreground.

✓ Lower the opacity for a subtle, translucent effect. Higher opacity replaces existing colors completely.

✓ Use a soft, round brush tip and regular hardness for smooth fills. Use harder tips for defined edges.

✓ Work on a new layer above your base artwork to preserve the original.

The Color Replacement Tool is great for quickly modifying colors or changing moods in a painting. Use it to shift lighting, make edits, or experiment with color schemes.

Mixer Brush Tool

The Mixer Brush replicates painting with traditional brushes and colors on a real canvas. Here are some tips:

✓ Select the **Mixer Brush** from the toolbar. It has an icon of a brush and paint tube.

✓ Pick foreground and background colors. The brush will blend them.

✓ Adjust the wetness to control how much color the brush holds. Higher wetness means more paint on the virtual brush.

✓ Set the **"Load: Clean Brush after Each Stroke"** option to continually add fresh paint from your color wells.

✓ Try different brush sizes and types. Bristle tips work well for mixing paint.

✓ Paint sweeps and strokes to mix colors on the canvas. Overlapping strokes will blend the shades realistically.

✓ Use the Clean Brush option to wipe away excess mixed color on the brush.

The Mixer Brush imitates real painting techniques. Use it when you want a fluid, blending brushwork in your digital art.

Eraser Tool

The Eraser Tool removes areas of color from your canvas:

✓ Select the Eraser Tool. It looks like a pink eraser icon.

✓ Pick an eraser type. Soft round brushes erase smoothly. Hard square tips give defined edges.

✓ Adjust size and hardness to control the erased area. Bigger sizes and lower hardness create softer edges.

✓ Set the opacity and flow. Lower settings are erased partially. Higher ones are erased.

✓ Click-drag your mouse or stylus over an area to erase. Hold Alt (on Windows) or Option (on Mac) as you erase to sample colors.

✓ Use a Layer Mask to non-destructively erase portions of a layer.

The Eraser is ideal for removing mistakes, creating textures, or clearing space for new paint. Use it cautiously, as you can't undo erasing on a flat canvas.

Brushes

Photoshop comes packed with brush presets tailored to different art styles. Here are some handy presets to try:

Hard round presets lay down solid colors with crisp edges, good for comics.

- ✓ Soft round presets blend and smear, nice for smoky textures.
- ✓ Scatter presets make speckled spatter strokes perfect for noise and spray effects.
- ✓ Charcoal presets emulate dusty, textured charcoal sketches.
- ✓ Ink presets produce liquid strokes like painting with a nib pen.

Creating Custom Brushes

You can make completely customized brushes to fit your artistic needs:

✓ Start with a base preset brush that has settings similar to what you want.

✓ Tweak settings like size, hardness, spacing, scatter, angle, and roundness to get the behavior you want.

✓ Shape the brush tip in the Brush Panel using options like pen pressure and tilt.

✓ Try making brush tips from your images for unique effects.

✓ Save your new brushes to add them to your library.

Managing Brush Libraries

As you collect more brushes, organize them using brush libraries:

✓ Make new library folders to group similar brushes, like oils or pencils.

✓ Rename libraries clearly so you can easily see their contents.

✓ Delete unused libraries to reduce clutter and free up space.

✓ Import libraries to access more brushes from online or other artists.

✓ Export libraries to back them up or share your brushes with others.

✓ Drag brushes between libraries to sort and arrange them.

Keep your brush libraries neat so you can always find the right brush fast while working on art.

Brush Settings

Customizing brushes allow you to paint digitally with more realistic and expressive strokes.

Brush Tip Shape

The brush tip determines the basic shape and line quality of your stroke. Try these tip shapes:

- ✓ Round for smooth, even strokes at any angle.
- ✓ Pointed for thin, tapered lines.
- ✓ Angled for flat, calligraphic lines.
- ✓ Scattered for spraying dots.
- ✓ Bristle for spreading color along the edges like a real brush.
- ✓ Grunge for textured, rough strokes.

Size

- ✓ Adjusting brush size controls the width and coverage of your strokes.
- ✓ Small sizes create thin, precise lines.
- ✓ Large sizes make thick, bold strokes.
- ✓ Use pressure sensitivity so size responds to pen pressure for natural variation.

✓ Varying size as you paint adds depth and dynamism to your brushwork.

Hardness

✓ The hardness setting determines stroke edge sharpness.

✓ At 100% hardness, strokes have crisp, well-defined edges.

✓ Lower hardness levels result in soft, blurred stroke edges.

✓ Use pressure sensitivity to transition between hard and soft as you paint.

✓ Hardness impacts the smoothness, texture, and blending behavior of your brush.

Spacing

✓ Spacing controls the gap between individual brush marks in a stroke.

✓ Tighter spacing flows together into continuous, unbroken lines.

✓ Larger spacing creates a dotted, dashed-line texture.

✓ Adjust spacing based on brush speed for smoother strokes at any pace.

✓ Vary spacing to create both smooth blends and textured, impressionistic effects.

Scattering

✓ Scattering distributes random specks of color within each brush stroke.

✓ Higher scatter levels add more speckles for denser, textured strokes.

✓ Lower scatter leaves strokes relatively solid and even.

✓ Use scattering to build up grainy textures with regular brushes.

✓ Add scattering to introduce more organic roughness and character to brush marks.

Texture

✓ Texture settings alter brush behavior to simulate painting on textured canvas.

✓ Increase texture scale for large visible bumps and grooves that warp strokes.

- ✓ Try textures like canvas, sandstone, and brick for natural media effects.

- ✓ Softer brushes show texture details. Hard brushes skate over them.

- ✓ Texture adds irregularity making strokes appear more dynamic and three-dimensional.

Painting Techniques

Painting on Layers

Painting on separate layers gives flexibility to independently edit parts of your artwork:

- ✓ Create new layers above your background layer to paint on.

- ✓ Use layer masks to hide/reveal portions non-destructively.

- ✓ Adjust layer order, blending, and opacity to composite your painting.

- ✓ Keep elements like line art or colors separate by layer.

✓ Layers let you easily erase, move, or change any part of a painting without damaging the rest.

Blending Modes

Change a layer's blending mode to interact with layers below it:

✓ Overlay combines colors while preserving highlights and shadows.

✓ Color burns to deepen shadows and contrasts.

✓ Lighten for luminous blending and color mixing.

✓ Darken to push darker tones into base layers.

Opacity/Flow

Lowering Opacity and Flow creates transparent, subtle brushstrokes:

✓ Opacity controls the transparency of the entire brush mark.

✓ Flow sets transparency only for the color applied.

✓ Use pressure sensitivity on these to vary faint/intense strokes naturally.

✓ Varying opacity/flow adds depth and realism to your painting process.

Wet Edges

Wet edges help blend strokes into smooth gradients:

✓ Enable **Wet Edges** in brush settings to partially mix paint as you go.

✓ Increase wetness to continue blending colors along the path of your stroke.

✓ Use Round brushes with Wet Edges to smoothly shade and render forms.

✓ Wet Edges replicate traditional blending techniques for continuous tone transitions.

Mixing Colors

Mix colors on your canvas to create rich secondary hues:

✓ Lay down adjacent strokes of different colors that overlap slightly.

✓ Use a Smudge tool to blend and mix the colors.

✓ Start with low flow to thinly build up the mixes gradually.

✓ On-canvas mixing provides natural, optically blended intermediate shades.

Smoothing and Smudging

Use tools like Smudge and Blur to soften harsh edges and blend colors:

✓ Smudge smears and mixes colors along the stroke direction.

✓ Blur filters diffuse edges and blend surrounding pixels.

✓ Use light pressure and short strokes to subtly integrate colors.

✓ Smoothing creates gradual value and hue transitions for cohesive paintings.

Cropping and Cloning

Cropping is one of the most basic but useful photo editing techniques. It allows you to trim away excess areas and focalize the core of your image. The Crop tool removes any parts of a photo that are not needed.

Cloning goes a step beyond cropping. It lets you patch over unwanted spots in a photo by sampling from other areas. Photoshop's cloning tools can replicate textures, colors, and lighting seamlessly.

Using the Crop Tool

The Crop tool allows you to trim edges from your photo. Here's how to use it:

- ✓ Open your image in Photoshop. The Crop tool is located in the toolbox.
- ✓ Click and drag over the area of the photo you want to keep. This will create crop borders.

- ✓ Adjust the crop borders as needed by dragging the handles on the edges and corners.
- ✓ Double-check that the area you want is within the crop selection.
- ✓ Click the checkmark button in the options bar to confirm the crop.
- ✓ The cropped photo will now show only the area you selected. Use the Crop tool to remove distracting elements and improve photo composition.

Cropping with Perspective

The Perspective Crop tool can fix crooked angles and skewed perspectives in photos. Follow these steps:

- ✓ Select the Perspective Crop tool from the toolbox.
- ✓ Draw a crop box over the image area you want to straighten.

✓ Click and drag on the corner handles to adjust the angle and perspective.

✓ When the crop box matches the photo angles you want, confirm the crop.

✓ The final cropped image will lose the skewed perspective and have corrected angles. The Perspective Crop is great for architectural photos or anytime you need to fix a tilted camera angle.

Cloning Areas with the Clone Stamp Tool

The Clone Stamp tool samples parts of a photo and replicates them in another area. Here's how to clone simple objects:

✓ Select the Clone Stamp tool from the toolbox.

✓ Alt-click (Option-click on Mac) on an area of your photo you want to clone from. This defines the sample source.

✓ Click or paint over another area to apply the cloned sample.

✓ Adjust the brush Size, Hardness, and Opacity to integrate the cloning effect.

✓ Switch sample sources and repeat cloning as needed.

Removing Imperfections with the Healing Brush

The Healing Brush tool works similarly to the Clone Stamp, but it blends your retouching into the target area. Follow these instructions:

✓ Select the Healing Brush from the toolbox.

✓ Alt-click (Option-click on Mac) on a source area with textures similar to the flaw you want to fix.

✓ Paint over the imperfection to replace it with the sampled textures.

✓ Adjust the brush Size and Hardness so changes blend in naturally.

✓ Switch sample points and make multiple passes if needed.

✓ The Healing Brush automatically matches tones and lighting. Use it to remove dust, blemishes, scratches, and other small imperfections.

Patching Up Areas with the Patch Tool

The Patch tool works like a large healing brush to replace entire areas. Here are the steps:

✓ Select the Patch tool from the toolbox.

✓ Draw a selection around the area you want to replace. Don't include sensitive edges.

✓ Click inside the selection and drag it over to a source area.

✓ Release to blend the new patch into place.

✓ Use the Patch tool sparingly, as dramatic patches may look edited. It excels at concealing wrinkles, scars, spots, and other unwanted areas.

Gradients

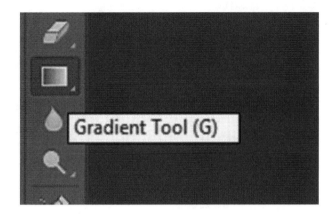

Gradients allow you to create smooth color blends, shadows, highlights, and other effects in your designs. Photoshop offers extensive gradient functionality through its Gradient tool, gradient presets, and gradient editing options.

Getting Started with Linear Gradients

Linear gradients blend two or more colors in a straight line. Follow these steps to create one:

✓ Select the **Gradient tool** from the Tools panel.

✓ In the **Options bar**, select a gradient preset or click the gradient sample to open the **Gradient Editor**.

✓ Choose the start and end colors for your gradient.

✓ On your document, click and drag to draw out the gradient.

✓ Adjust the gradient length, angle, and opacity as needed.

✓ Apply a **Gradient Overlay** layer style to add gradients to text or vector shapes.

✓ Linear gradients are great for simple backgrounds, subtle color washes, and sleek modern effects.

Using Radial Gradients

Radial gradients radiate out in a circular pattern from a central point. Here's how to make one:

✓ Select the Gradient tool and set foreground/background colors.

✓ Select the Radial gradient option in the **Options** bar.

✓ Click on the document where you want the gradient centered.

✓ Drag outward to define the gradient radius and shape.

✓ Adjust the gradient's bounds, opacity, or angles if desired.

✓ Apply to shapes using **Layer Styles > Gradient Overlay**.

✓ Radial gradients create spheres of color and are perfect for lighting effects, focal points, and abstract backdrops.

Applying Gradient Presets

Photoshop comes packed with preset gradients ready to use in one click. Access and use them this way:

✓ Open the **Gradient** presets panel by clicking the gradient sample in the **Options** bar.

✓ Scroll through the different presets to preview color patterns.

✓ Click on a preset to select it. This replaces your current gradient.

✓ Draw the preset gradient out on your canvas.

✓ Adjust the gradient's length, angle, scale, or reverse option.

✓ Save new presets by clicking the **"New"** icon in the panel.

✓ Gradient presets make quick work of applying professional effects to any project.

Customizing Gradients in the Editor

For complete control, you can customize gradients in the Gradient Editor panel:

✓ Open the panel using the gradient sample in the Options bar.

✓ Select the gradient you want to edit or load a preset.

- ✓ Click below the gradient bar to add extra color points.
- ✓ Adjust colors and positioning by dragging color stops left/right.
- ✓ Change opacity by lowering alpha points between stops.
- ✓ Set blend modes for more artistic gradients.
- ✓ Save your custom gradients to reuse later.
- ✓ The Gradient Editor provides unlimited options for crafting your signature gradient effects.

Applying Gradients for Maximum Impact

Here are some pro tips for using gradients effectively in your Photoshop designs:

- ✓ Use Layer Styles to apply gradients non-destructively to layers.
- ✓ Overlay gradients on photos to create color tints and washes.
- ✓ Boost contrast by blending dark and light-toned gradients.
- ✓ Mimic lighting with radial gradients pointed from a top corner.

✓ Stack multiple subtle gradients on separate layers for dimension.

✓ Skew or warp gradients using Transform tools for abstract effects.

✓ Brush on gradients with the Gradient tool for hand-painted texture.

✓ With a little creativity, gradients can bring any flat design to life with dynamic colors.

Patterns

Patterns allow you to fill layers and vector shapes with repeating preset designs.

Photoshop includes a range of checkered, geometric, nature, and abstract pattern presets. Follow these steps to use them:

✓ Open the Patterns preset panel by clicking on the pattern thumbnail in the Options bar.

✓ Scroll through the different pattern thumbnails to preview available presets.

- ✓ Click on a pattern to select it as your foreground fill.
- ✓ On your document, use the Paint Bucket tool or a fill layer to apply the pattern.
- ✓ Adjust the pattern scale and position to fit your document size and layout.
- ✓ With just a click, preset patterns provide instant background fill textures for posters, cards, webpages, and more.

Creating Custom Patterns

You can generate your unique patterns from images. Here's how:

- ✓ Open or create a new document with the image you want to pattern.
- ✓ Select just a small portion of the image to use as the repeating pattern.
- ✓ Copy the selection.
- ✓ Open the Pattern preset panel and click **"New"** to create a blank pattern.

✓ Paste your copied selection into the blank pattern slot.

✓ Set the pattern size to match your selection width/height.

✓ Click the DONE button to finalize the new custom pattern.

✓ Apply your custom pattern using the Paint Bucket tool or as a fill layer.

✓ Creating quality patterns takes experimentation. Play with angles, arrangement, and color combinations. Abstract patterns work best.

Scaling and Positioning Patterns

One advantage of patterns is they are quick to edit and adjust:

✓ Scale patterns up or down using the Pattern Fill layer style options.

✓ Rotate patterns in 90-degree increments with the layer style angle setting.

- ✓ Offset patterns by specifying X/Y percentages in the layer style interface.
- ✓ Use the Snap to Origin option to reset pattern positioning.
- ✓ Align multiple patterns perfectly by linking pattern layers.
- ✓ Edit the original pattern image to update linked instances.
- ✓ Properly scaled and aligned, patterns create the illusion of one continuous design.

Creative Uses for Patterns

Patterns aren't just for basic fills. Here are some creative ways to implement patterns:

- ✓ Use low-opacity layers to add natural texture to photos.
- ✓ Blend colored patterns with Soft Light and Overlay blend modes.
- ✓ Brush patterns with the Pattern Stamp tool for painterly effects.

✓ Add patterns sparingly to accent key areas and leading lines.

✓ Mix large and small patterns on separate layers for dimension.

✓ Apply inverted patterns with Difference or Exclusion blends.

✓ Mask patterns to uncover and highlight the subject matter.

CHAPTER TEN

Basic Retouching

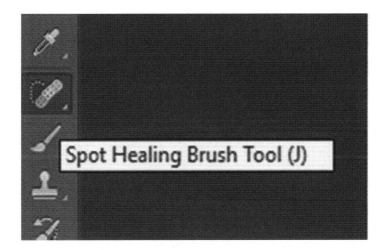

With Photoshop 2024, you can make almost any edit or enhancement imaginable to improve the look of your photos.

Cropping

One of the most basic and useful retouching tasks is cropping your image to improve its composition. Here's how:

✓ Open the image you want to crop in Photoshop.

✓ Select the Crop tool from the toolbar on the left. It looks like a square with the bottom right corner missing.

✓ Click and drag your mouse on the image to select the area you want to keep. Photoshop will shade out the part of the image to be cropped.

✓ Adjust the crop area as needed by dragging the edges and corners.

✓ When satisfied, click the check mark in the options bar at the top to confirm the crop.

✓ Cropping removes any unnecessary background details or distracting elements to better frame your main subject. Cropping also allows you to change the shape and size of your image.

Straightening

If your image wasn't shot straight and has a slight tilt, the Straighten tool can fix it:

✓ Select the Straighten tool from the toolbar (nested under the Crop tool).

✓ Click and drag along a line in your image that should be horizontal or vertical. Photoshop draws a guiding line.

✓ When the guideline is aligned, release the mouse. The image will be rotated automatically to straighten it.

✓ Use the Crop tool to remove any white edges created by the rotation.

✓ Straightening the horizon or architecture lines makes a huge difference in the overall appearance of an image.

Red Eye Removal

Red-eye occurs when the camera's flash reflects off the retina in the back of the eye, making the pupil appear red. To remove it:

✓ Zoom in close on any eyes that have red eyes in your image.

✓ Select the Red Eye tool from the toolbar on the left side.

- ✓ Click once on each red eye. Photoshop will automatically replace the red with a natural black pupil.
- ✓ If needed, adjust the pupil size with the slider in the options bar.
- ✓ The Red Eye tool offers a quick way to correct this common issue and make your subjects look their best.

Spot Healing

The Spot Healing brush lets you easily remove small imperfections like blemishes, dust spots, power lines, and more:

- ✓ Zoom in close on the area containing the unwanted spot.
- ✓ Select the Spot Healing brush from the toolbar (nested under the Healing Brush).
- ✓ Adjust the brush size as needed to cover the spot.
- ✓ Click on the spot once. Photoshop will sample from surrounding pixels to cover it.

✓ Check that it blends well and touch up as needed.

✓ With just a click, the Spot Healing brush can make spots, dust, and other small defects disappear while retaining surrounding detail and texture.

Clone Stamp

For retouching larger areas or objects you want to remove entirely, use the Clone Stamp:

✓ Zoom in on the area to retouch.

✓ Select the Clone Stamp from the toolbar.

✓ Alt-click (Option-click on Mac) on an area of your photo to set the sampling point.

✓ Adjust brush size and hardness as needed.

✓ Click and paint over the area to cover it with the sampled pixels.

✓ Release Alt to reset the sampling point, then repeat steps 3-5 as needed.

✓ The Clone Stamp duplicates and paints over any section of your image, letting you seamlessly cover and erase imperfections.

Healing Brush

Similar to the Clone Stamp, the Healing Brush blends with surrounding texture and lighting for a more natural look:

- ✓ Zoom in on the area to retouch.
- ✓ Select the Healing Brush from the toolbar.
- ✓ Alt-click (Option-click on Mac) to set a sampling point.
- ✓ Adjust brush size and hardness.
- ✓ Click and paint over the area to heal. Photoshop will blend it with the lighting and texture around it.
- ✓ Release Alt and reset sampling points as needed.
- ✓ Use the Healing Brush when you want to cover flaws while maintaining a natural look that isn't obvious.

Distortion Tools

Filter	3D	View	Window	Help	
Last Filter					Ctrl+F
Convert for Smart Filters					
Filter Gallery...					
Adaptive Wide Angle...					Alt+Shift+Ctrl+A
Camera Raw Filter...					Shift+Ctrl+A
Lens Correction...					Shift+Ctrl+R
Liquify...					Shift+Ctrl+X

One of the fun and creative ways to edit images is by distorting, warping, and morphing elements in your photo. Photoshop 2024 includes a variety of powerful distortion tools that let you stretch, pinch, twist, and reshape your images in unique ways.

Liquify Filter

The Liquify filter lets you distort images in fully customizable ways:

✓ Open an image and select **Filter > Liquify** from the top menu.

✓ Select any of the distortion tools on the right like Warp, Bloat, Pucker, etc.

✓ Adjust the brush size, density, and pressure as needed.

✓ Paint over the areas of your image you want to distort. The effect is applied in real-time.

✓ Use the Reconstruct tool to dial back changes or restore the original image.

✓ When satisfied, click OK to apply the Liquify filter.

Warp Transform

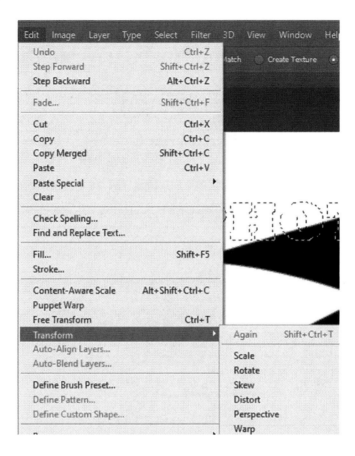

Photoshop's Warp transforms offer preset distortion effects:

- ✓ Select the layer you want to transform.
- ✓ Go to **Edit > Transform > Warp.**
- ✓ Select a warp style like Arc, Flag, Twist, etc.
- ✓ Adjust the sliders and handles to control the strength and shape.

✓ Click the check mark when finished to commit the transform.

✓ Try out different Warp transform styles on elements like text or shapes to bend, curve, and manipulate them.

Perspective Transform

The Perspective transform simulates depth and perspective changes:

✓ Select the layer, object, or text.

✓ Go to **Edit > Transform > Perspective**.

✓ Click and drag the corner handles to skew and distort perspective.

✓ Adjust the grid lines to change the vanishing points.

✓ Click the check mark when satisfied to apply.

✓ Perspective transforms are great for manipulating objects, text, and shapes to add exaggerated perspective and depth.

Scale and Skew

For quick and easy transformations, use the Scale and Skew options:

- ✓ Select the layer, object, or text to transform.
- ✓ Go to **Edit > Transform** and select **Scale** or **Skew**.
- ✓ Adjust the handles and numerical inputs to stretch, squash, and slant the selection.
- ✓ Hold Shift as you transform to retain proper proportions.
- ✓ Confirm the changes by clicking the check mark.
- ✓ The Scale and Skew transform provides a simple way to squash, stretch, and tilt elements on both the vertical and horizontal axes.

Camera Raw

Camera Raw is Photoshop's raw image processing engine. It provides non-destructive editing of raw files to correct color, adjust exposure, reduce noise, and sharpen images before further editing.

White Balance

Correct color casts and set proper white balance:

- Open a raw photo, then click the **Basic** tab in Camera Raw.
- Select the **White Balance** tool.
- Click on an area that should be neutral white or gray.
- The Temperature and Tint sliders will adjust to the correct color.
- Fine-tune as needed to remove color casts.
- Proper white balance removes unrealistic color caused by light source temperature. Set it first for accurate colors.

Noise Reduction

Reduce unwanted luminance and color noise:

- In the **Detail** tab, adjust Luminance to reduce luminance noise.

- Increase Luminance Detail to preserve details if needed.
- Adjust the Color slider to remove color chroma noise while maintaining saturation.
- Use Color Detail if reducing Color introduces hue shifts.
- Controlling noise gives you clean, smooth images while retaining detail and color fidelity.

Sharpening

Add edge sharpness and detail back to images:

- In the **Detail** tab, increase the Amount to add sharpening.
- Adjust the Radius higher to sharpen larger edges.
- Reduce Masking to apply sharpening to noisy areas like skies.
- Use the Detail slider for enhanced fine edge definition if needed.

- Strategic sharpening enhances edge definition and focuses while avoiding artifacting.

Geometry Corrections

Fix lens flaws like distortion and perspective:

- Switch to the **Lens Corrections** tab.
- Check the Enable **Lens Profile Corrections** box.
- Adjust distortion sliders like Vertical to fix shape distortion.
- Use the Transform sliders to fix perspective issues.
- Correcting lens geometry compensates for aberrations and perspective flaws.

Panorama Stitching

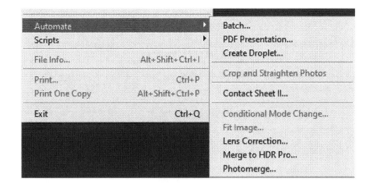

Photoshop 2024 includes panorama stitching capabilities to merge multiple photos into one seamless panoramic image. By taking a series of overlapping photos and combining them, you can create ultra-wide landscapes or 360-degree panoramic views.

Photomerge

The easiest way to stitch a panorama is using Photoshop's Photomerge:

Open all the individual photos you want to stitch into one panorama.

1. Go to **File >Automate >Photomerge**.

2. Select either Auto or Perspective layout mode. Auto works best for simpler panoramas.

3. Click OK. Photoshop will automatically combine the images.

4. The resulting panorama will open in a new document, ready to export.

5. Photomerge takes care of aligning and blending your images to create the full panorama with minimal effort.

Auto-Blending Layers

For more control, stitch manually using auto-blend layers:

1. Place your panorama photos on layers in a single document.

2. Arrange them in the correct left-to-right or top-down order.

3. Ensure some overlap between the edges of each layer.

4. Right-click the layers and choose Auto-Blend Layers.

5. Select Panorama for the blend mode.

6. Photoshop will automatically stitch and mask the layers.

7. Auto-blend seamlessly merges overlapping layers into a cohesive panorama.

Manual Blending

Manually retouch and blend layers to create a flawless panorama:

1. Follow steps 1-3 above but skip the auto-blend.

2. Add layer masks to blend the seams between layers.

3. Paint with black to hide bad overlaps and blend manually.

4. Use the Clone Stamp tool to copy good edges and patch seams.

5. Erase ghosting, adjust tones, and touch up other flaws.

6. Flatten the image when done editing the panorama layers.

7. Blending manually takes more work but allows full control over creating a perfectly seamless panorama.

CHAPTER ELEVEN

Layers

Layers are like transparent sheets stacked on top of each other, with each layer containing separate image information that can be edited independently.

Creating New Layers

There are several ways to create new layers:

Layer panel: Click the "Create a new layer" button at the bottom of the Layers panel.

Keyboard shortcut: Press Control + Shift + N (Windows) or Command + Shift + N (Mac).

Copy/paste: Copying and pasting an image or selection automatically creates a new layer.

Dragging files: Dragging images into an open Photoshop document adds them as new layers.

Importing files: Check the "Import as new layer" box when importing files to add them as layers.

New layers are created above the currently selected layer. Name your layers clearly for easy editing.

Moving Layers

To move a layer in the stacking order:

➢ Select the layer you want to move.
➢ Drag it up or down to the desired position in the Layers panel. The cursor will display a bracket indicating the new position.

You can also use the following shortcuts:

➢ Control + [(Windows) or Command + [(Mac) - Move layer down

➢ Control +] (Windows) or Command +] (Mac)-
Move layer up

➢ Moving layers change their stacking order
and how they interact with layers below
them.

Changing Layer Stacking Order

The stacking order of layers determines which
content appears in front and which is behind. Top
layers obscure parts of those below them.

To change a layer's stacking order:

➢ Select the layer you want to rearrange.

➢ Drag and drop within the Layers panel to the
new position.

Alternatively, use the Layer menu options to:

➢ Bring layer forward

➢ Send layer backward

➢ Move the layer to the topmost position

➢ Move the layer to the bottom position

➢ Correct stacking order is crucial for your final
image.

Grouping Layers

Grouping layers combine them while still preserving their editability. This helps organize related layers.

To group layers:

> ➢ Select the layers to group in the Layers panel.
> ➢ Click the "Create a new group" button at the bottom of the panel.
> ➢ Name the group.

To edit a single layer within a group:

> ➢ Click the arrow next to the group to expand it.
> ➢ Click the layer to select it.
> ➢ Make your edits.
> ➢ Grouping helps manage complex documents with many layers.

Linking Layers

Linking layers causes them to move together as one unit:

> ➢ Select the layers to link in the Layers panel.

➢ Click the **"Link Layers"** button near the bottom of the panel.

➢ Now when you move one of the linked layers, all linked layers will move together.

➢ To unlink layers, select them and click the "Unlink Layers" button.

Locking Layers

Locking prevents accidental changes to a layer. Locked layers are not editable.

To lock or unlock in the Layers panel:

➢ Click the empty box - Unlocked

➢ Click the lock icon - Locked

➢ You can also select a layer and use the Layer > Lock command.

➢ Lock important layers before making widespread edits to protect them.

Blending Layers

Blending modes control how the pixels on a layer interact with layers below it. The default is Normal.

To blend layers:

> ➢ Select the layer to adjust.
> ➢ In the Layers panel, choose a blending mode from the dropdown menu.

Some common blending modes:

Multiply - Darkens image. Good for shadows.

Screen - Lightens image. Good for highlights.

Overlay - Combines Multiply and Screen.

Difference - Compares layers and displays inverted results.

Experiment with blending modes using duplicate layers to get different effects.

Merging and Flattening Layers

When you're done editing layers, you can:

> ➢ Merge layers to combine them into one new layer.
> ➢ Flatten the image to merge all layers into the background layer.

➢ This simplifies your document. Merged layers can no longer be edited separately.

➢ To merge or flatten, right-click a layer and choose the desired option.

Adjustment Layers

Adjustment layers apply color and tonal adjustments to the layers below them.

Let's go through using each of these adjustment layers.

Brightness/Contrast Adjustment

To quickly adjust image brightness and contrast:

➢ Click **Layer > New Adjustment Layer > Brightness/Contrast**.

➢ In the New Layer dialog box, click OK.

➢ Adjust brightness and contrast sliders.

➢ Click OK when done.

➢ This adds an editable adjustment layer. Lowering contrast and increasing brightness is great for a faded look.

Hue/Saturation Adjustment

To shift all image hues and color saturation:

➢ Click **Layer > New Adjustment Layer > Hue/Saturation**.

➢ Select color channel: Master, Reds, Yellows, etc.

➢ Drag sliders to alter hues and saturation.

➢ Click OK when finished.

➢ Use this for color correction or stylized effects. Reduce saturation for a muted look.

Black & White Adjustment

Converting to black and white:

➢ Click **Layer > New Adjustment Layer > Black & White.**

➢ Adjust color sliders to control conversion.

➢ Click OK when done.

➢ Increase yellows/reds to darken the sky. Boost blues for whiter clouds. Customize for best results.

Photo Filter Adjustment

Adding color filter effects:

➢ Click **Layer > New Adjustment Layer > Photo Filter**.

➢ Pick a filter color. Adjust density.

➢ Click OK to apply.

➢ Try warming or cooling filters. Use at low density for subtle color casts.

Channel Mixer Adjustment

Fine-tuning channels for custom effects:

➤ Click **Layer > New Adjustment Layer > Channel Mixer**.

➤ Adjust channel sliders.

➤ Click OK when finished.

➤ Great for advanced control over black & white conversion. Also useful for creative color effects.

Working with Multiple Adjustments

➤ Use clipping masks to apply adjustments to only specific layers below.

➤ Experiment with adjustment layer stacking order.

➤ Lower opacity to reduce effect strength.

➤ Change blend mode—Overlay can intensify contrast.

➤ Disable/enable adjustment layers to view before/after.

➢ Adjustments combined with masks give you endless creative options.

File Compositing

Compositing refers to combining multiple files—including images, videos, text, and more—into one cohesive final document.

Placing Files in Photoshop

To place a file into an open Photoshop document:

➢ Obtain files to composite—photos, illustrations, text, video, etc.

➢ In Photoshop, navigate to **File > Place Embedded** or **Place Linked**.

➢ Browse to select your file and click Place.

➢ Position the placed file. Click the checkmark icon to commit placement.

➢ Placed files appear as new layers for easy editing. Adjust blending modes or opacity to integrate placed elements.

Embedding Files

Embedding fully incorporates external files into your Photoshop project. To embed:

➢ Follow the place file steps above.

➢ In the Import options, select Embed.

➢ Click OK.

The file becomes embedded within the PSD, growing its size. Upsides:

➢ Self-contained Photoshop file

➢ Content always available

➢ Easier file management

Downsides:

➢ Large file sizes

➢ Can't edit original external files

Linking Files

Linking connects external files to your PSD without embedding. To link:

➢ Follow the place file steps.

➢ In the Import options, select Link.

228

➢ Click OK.

This maintains a connection to the original file. Benefits:

➢ Smaller Photoshop file size

➢ Ability to edit original files later

➢ Dynamic updates when external files change

➢ The downside is needing the linked files to view/edit the PSD. Manage links carefully.

Managing Linked Files

With linked files, you'll need to manage connections:

➢ Move linked files together with the PSD.

➢ Package files using the **File > Package** command.

➢ Update modified links using **Layer > Update Linked Layers**.

➢ Break links to embedded content with **Layer > Embed Linked**.

➢ Monitor Photoshop's missing link warnings. Embed or relink as needed for seamless compositing.

Blending Composite Elements

Use layer blending options to polish your composite:

➢ Adjust opacity to tweak visibility.

➢ Change blending mode—screen works well for brightening.

➢ Use layer masks to finesse edges and blend.

➢ Add adjustment layers to match color and tone.

Merging Layers

Merging in Photoshop combines layers or groups into a single new layer or image. This simplifies your document's layer structure and permanently fuses elements.

Merging Layers

To selectively merge layers:

> ➢ In the Layers panel, select the layers to merge.
>
> ➢ Right-click and choose Merge Layers.
>
> ➢ Name the new merged layer.
>
> ➢ You can also use **Layer > Merge Layers**.
>
> ➢ This combines pixels while preserving effects like opacity and masks. Great for streamlining.

Merging Visible Layers

To merge all visible layers in your document:

> ➢ Hide any layers you want to keep separate.
>
> ➢ Click **Layer > Merge Visible**.
>
> ➢ Name the resulting layer.
>
> ➢ Merged visible layers get flattened together into one new layer. Useful for consolidating edits.

Flattening the Image

Flattening merges all layers into a background:

> ➢ Ensure all desired edits are done first.

➢ Go to **Layer > Flatten Image**.

➢ This permanently fuses all layers and content into one background layer.

➢ Do this when fully done editing individual layers. Flattened pixels can't be changed.

Smart Merging Strategies

➢ Group related layers first, then merge the group.

➢ Duplicate layers before merging to allow going back.

➢ Merge adjustment layers at the end to preserve edits.

➢ Add layer masks before merging to blend content.

➢ Name merged layers meaningfully for easy reference.

➢ Merging well keeps your document organized as edits build up.

When to Avoid Merging

Avoid merging layers when:

➢ You want to retain the editability of separate layers.

➢ Working on complex compositions.

➢ Unsure if additional changes are needed.

➢ Multiple people are collaborating.

➢ Wait until edits are finalized before decisively merging.

CHAPTER TWELVE

Filter Basics

Filters are a tool for applying effects and adjustments to your images in Photoshop.

Accessing Filters

Photoshop's wide range of filters is located in the Filter menu at the top of the screen. To access them:

> ➤ Open an image in Photoshop.
> ➤ Go to **Filter > Filter Gallery** to open the Filter Gallery window. This provides a preview of

how filters will look when applied to your image.

➢ To access a specific filter category, select it from the list on the left side of the Filter Gallery window. For example, click on Artistic to view artistic filters.

➢ To apply a filter, click on its name and adjust any settings in the preview pane. Then click OK to apply it to your image.

➢ You can also access certain common filters quickly from the Filter menu itself, like Blur, Sharpen, Distort, and Noise. Select a filter from the menu to apply it.

Applying Standard Filters

Photoshop includes dozens of filters divided into categories like Artistic, Blur, Distort, Noise, Pixelate, Render, Sharpen, Sketch, Stylize, Texture, and Video. Here are some examples of what standard filters can do:

➤ Blur filters like Gaussian Blur soften sharp edges and details. Use them to create depth of field or motion blur effects.

➤ With 'sharpen' filters like Unsharp Mask, you can make details pop and reduce image noise and grain.

➤ The Pixelate category lets you mosaic or color block images for a retro or abstract look.

➤ Distort filters like Pinch and Polar Coordinates create funhouse mirror effects by shifting pixels.

➤ Artistic filters can transform a photo into a painting, drawing, or graphic style. Examples include Cutout, Palette Knife, and Watercolor.

To apply any filter:

➤ Open an image and access the filter you want to use from the Filter menu or Filter Gallery.

➤ Adjust settings like blur amount or brush size in the filter's options pane.

➢ Click OK to apply the filter to your image. You can adjust filter strength after applying by going to **Edit > Fade Filter**.

Using Third-Party Filters

In addition to Photoshop's built-in filters, you can get access to hundreds more creative filters by installing third-party filter packs. Some popular sources are Filter Forge, Flaming Pear, and ON1.

Third-party filters function just like Photoshop's regular filters. To use them:

➢ Download and install the filter pack you want. Follow the provider's installation instructions.

➢ Restart Photoshop if prompted. The new filters will now appear in the Filter menu or Filter Gallery.

➢ Apply them to images just like you would regular filters. Note that some third-party filters have more customizable settings and options.

➢ With third-party filters, the possibilities are endless! You can introduce unique textures, lighting effects, distortions, color adjustments, and more that aren't available in Photoshop by default.

Using Smart Filters for Non-Destructive Editing

One limitation with regular filters is that they permanently alter your image pixels. Fortunately, Smart Filters provides a non-destructive filtering method.

When you apply a filter as a Smart Filter, Photoshop adds it as a separate layer rather than merging it with the image. This allows you to adjust, delete, or hide the filter at any time.

Here is how to use Smart Filters:

Convert your base image layer to a Smart Object. Go to **Layer > Smart Objects > Convert to Smart Object.**

Now when you apply a filter, check the box for **"Smart Filters"** in the filter options pane before clicking OK.

The filter will be applied as a Smart Filter instead of altering your original image layer.

To edit the Smart Filter, double-click its layer thumbnail to re-open the filter options.

Smart Filters give you more flexibility and control when using filters in your workflows.

Neural Filters

Photoshop neural filters utilize artificial intelligence to apply complex edits and adjustments to images with just a few clicks.

Accessing Neural Filters

To start using neural filters, you first need to locate them within Photoshop's workspace. Here's how to access them:

➢ Open an image in Photoshop. Neural filters can be applied to layers, so it's recommended to start with a multilayered document.

➢ Click on the Layers tab to view your layers palette.

➢ At the top of the Layers palette, click on the **"Add filter"** button (it appears as a star icon).

➢ This will open the Filter Gallery on the right side of the screen.

➢ At the top of the Filter Gallery, click on the drop-down menu next to **"Filters"** and select **"Neural Filters."**

➢ The Neural Filters options will now appear in the **Filter Gallery**. From here, you can choose which effect to apply.

Applying Specific Neural Filters

Photoshop currently includes five different neural filters. Here's an overview of each effect and how to apply them:

Colorize Filter

The Colorize filter adds color to a black-and-white image while preserving the original luminance. To use it:

With the Neural Filters menu open, click on **"Colorize."**

Choose a color scheme from the dropdown menu. Vivid applies punchy, saturated hues. Subtle provides softer, muted colors.

Adjust the Amount slider to control color intensity.

Click OK to apply the filter to your layer.

Landscape Mixer Filter

This filter blends multiple landscape photos into one cohesive image. To use it:

➢ Select **"Landscape Mixer"** from the Neural Filters menu.

➢ Click "Add layer" to select 2-5 landscape photos from your computer.

➢ Check the Invert box to switch foreground and background layers.

➢ Adjust the Target Photo slider to control blend intensity.

➢ Click OK to merge the layers into one landscape image.

Smart Portrait Filter

The Smart Portrait filter realistically adjusts the lighting on faces. To use it:

➢ Choose **"Smart Portrait"** from the Neural Filters menu.

➢ Adjust the lighting position by clicking and dragging the sun icon.

➢ Fine-tune Light Brightness and Contrast sliders.

➢ Click OK to apply the lighting effect.

Style Transfer Filter

This filter transfers the style of one image onto the content of another image. To use it:

➢ Select "Style Transfer" from the Neural Filters menu.

➢ Click "Add style image" and choose a photo with the desired artistic style.

➢ Adjust the Transfer slider to control effect intensity.

➢ Click OK to apply the style transfer to your photo.

Superzoom Filter

The Superzoom filter increases image resolution for detailed enlargements. To use it:

➢ Choose "Superzoom" from the Neural Filters menu.

➢ Click and drag to draw a rectangle over the area you want to enlarge.

➢ Adjust the Model and Area sliders to refine the zoom.

➢ Click OK to magnify the selected region.

Tips for Best Results

➢ Neural filters work best on images with good lighting and focus. Avoid applying them to low-quality photos.

➢ Try adjusting filter settings instead of using presets for more control over the effect.

➢ Use Smart Filters to apply filters as non-destructive adjustment layers.

➢ Stack multiple neural filters to create unique image effects.

CHAPTER THIRTEEN

Batch Processing

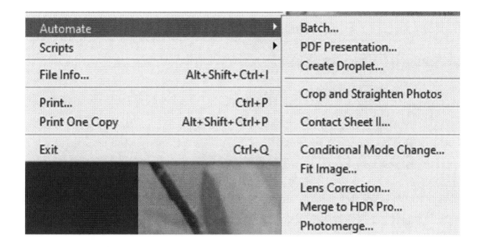

Batch processing in Photoshop allows you to automate the editing of multiple photos by applying image adjustments, resizing, converting formats, and more in one action. This saves huge amounts of time compared to manually editing each photo one by one.

Batch Command

The Batch command allows you to batch process by using an existing action:

➤ Open the Actions panel and create a new action with the edits you want to apply.

➤ Go to **File > Automate > Batch**.

➤ Set the Action dropdown to your new action.

➤ Click the Choose button to select the source folder of files.

➤ Specify the destination folder for the processed photos.

➤ Check any options like **'Override Action "Open" Commands'**.

➤ Click OK to process the batch.

Create Droplet

To batch process by dragging and dropping files onto an icon:

➤ Go to **File > Automate > Create Droplet**.

➤ Choose the set of actions/adjustments to apply.

➢ Select a destination folder for the output files.

➢ Specify saving options like file type, quality, etc.

➢ Click OK to create the droplet on your desktop.

➢ Simply drag photos onto the droplet icon to batch-process them.

Variables

Variables help you store customizable values that can be reused in actions. By using variables, you can build flexible actions that adapt to different parameters each time the action is run.

Creating Variables

To create a text or numeric variable:

➢ Open the **Actions** panel in Photoshop. Click the menu icon in the top right.

➢ **Select 'New** Variable...' to open the **New Variable** dialog box.

➢ Name the variable something descriptive like "File_Name" or "Border_Thickness".

➢ Set the Type to Text or Numeric depending on your needs.

➢ Enter a Default Value if desired. This sets the initial value.

➢ Click OK to create the variable.

Using Variables in Actions

Once created, variables can be added to actions:

➢ Begin recording a new action.

➢ For text variables, use the Set command to set the value. For numerics, use the Set Numeric Value command.

➢ Insert the variable name by clicking the Insert Menu Item button and selecting the variable.

➢ When playing back the action, you'll be prompted to enter the variable value.

You can also use variables in batch processes:

➢ In the **Batch** or **Image Processor** dialog, click the underlined text next to **'Source'** and **'Destination'**.

➢ Select your variable from the list to dynamically insert the values into filenames or folders.

Data Sets

With Data Sets, you can import and use tabular data from CSV or TXT files for dynamic batch processing. By leveraging data sets, you can process multiple files based on matching data columns to file names or other attributes.

Import Data Sets

To import a data set:

➢ Click the menu icon in the Actions panel and select 'Import Data Set...'.

➢ Navigate to and select your CSV or TXT data file. The first row should be column headers.

➢ Specify the encoding and column delimiter if necessary.

➢ Click OK to import the data set. It will appear in the Actions panel menu.

➢ You can also export an existing data set as a CSV file from the Actions panel menu.

Using Data Sets in Batch Processing

With a data set imported, you can leverage it for batch processing:

➢ Set up your batch process through **File > Automate > Batch or Image Processor.**

➢ Click the underlined **'Source'** text and select your imported data set from the menu.

➢ Set the Source Column to the column in your data set that matches image filenames or attributes.

➢ Repeat for the Destination and any other settings you want to pull from the data set.

➢ Run the batch process to apply actions dynamically based on the data set.

Presets

Presets allow you to save and quickly apply commonly used settings for tools, styles, brushes, swatches, patterns, contours, custom shapes, and more. Using presets can improve consistency across projects and significantly speed up your workflow.

Using Tool Presets

To apply a tool preset:

➢ Select the tool you want to use, like the Rectangle or Brush tool.

➢ Click the tool presets panel icon to open it if not already visible.

➢ Click a preset thumbnail image to select it.

➢ Adjust options like size if needed.

➢ Use the tool. Settings will be applied from the preset.

Making New Tool Presets

To save tool settings as a preset:

➢ Select the desired tool and customize settings as needed.

➢ Click the tool presets panel menu.

➢ Select **'New Tool Preset'** and give it a name.

➢ The new preset will appear in the panel ready to apply.

Managing Presets

You can organize presets in the Preset Manager:

➢ Choose Edit > Preset Manager to open the manager.

➢ Select a preset type on the left like Brushes or Styles.

➢ Click buttons to load, save, or delete presets.

➢ Drag presets into folders to organize.

Contact Sheet II

Contact Sheet II is a handy built-in Photoshop tool for automatically generating contact sheets - pages with thumbnails of multiple images arranged in a grid. This saves hours of tedious manual layout work.

Layout Design

To set up your contact sheet layout:

Go to **File > Automate > Contact Sheet II**.

➢ Select your folder of images.

➢ Choose the size, resolution, and color mode.

➢ Pick a layout like rows and columns. Adjust spacing as needed.

➢ Select options like **'Include All Open Files'** to add open images.

➢ Choose a font and size for captions if desired.

Output Options

To finalize your contact sheet:

> ➤ Check any output options like flattening layers or adding a background color.
>
> ➤ Select the file type and quality settings to save as.
>
> ➤ Choose a destination folder location.
>
> ➤ Name your contact sheet file.
>
> ➤ Click OK to generate the automated PDF or image file.

Saving Templates

To save a custom layout as a template:

> ➤ Set up your desired layout in the Contact Sheet II dialog box.
>
> ➤ Click the Save button at the top next to the preset dropdown.
>
> ➤ Name your template preset and click Save.
>
> ➤ Your layout is now reachable from the Preset dropdown for reuse.

PDF Presentation

The PDF Presentation tool makes it easy to turn images and text into slideshow-style PDF presentations. This allows you to quickly create elegant and interactive portfolios, photo stories, image galleries, and more.

Slide Layouts

To set up your PDF slides:

- ➢ Go to **File > Automate > PDF Presentation**.
- ➢ Select your images or PSD files to include.
- ➢ Choose a preset layout like **'Full Screen'** or customize dimensions.
- ➢ Pick a background color if desired.
- ➢ Check 'Show Grid' to enable perfect alignment.
- ➢ Arrange images and text boxes into slides.

Transitions

To add transitions between slides:

➢ Click the Transition tab in the PDF Presentation dialog box.

➢ Choose a transition type like 'Dissolve' or 'Wipe'.

➢ Adjust transition direction if applicable.

➢ Set transition duration in seconds.

Output Options

To finalize and save your PDF:

➢ Go to the Output tab to select quality and view options.

➢ Pick **'View After Saving'** to preview the presentation.

➢ Choose a save location and filename.

➢ Click Save to generate the interactive PDF presentation.

CHAPTER FOUREEN

3D Basics

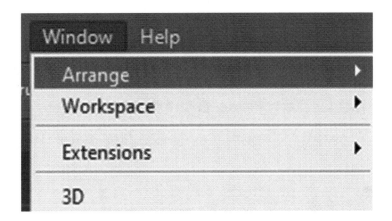

With a few simple tools and options, you can start incorporating 3D images into your Photoshop 2024 designs and enhance your creative projects.

Importing 3D Models

The first step to working with 3D in Photoshop is to import a 3D model file into your document. Photoshop supports various common 3D formats, such as .OBJ, .3DS, and .STL files. You can download 3D models from online sources, create your own using modeling software, or convert files from other programs.

Once you have your 3D model file, here's how to import it:

> Open the document you want to place the 3D model in.
> Go to **File > Place Embedded**.
> Browse to your 3D model file, select it, and click Place.
> Choose the plane you want to place the model on. The default is the center of the canvas.
> The 3D model will now appear on its layer in your Photoshop document, ready to be edited and customized.

Placing 3D Models

When you import a 3D model into Photoshop, it will be placed at a default size in the center of your document. You can easily move, rotate, and resize the imported 3D object to customize its placement.

Here are some tips for placing 3D models:

➢ Use the Move tool to drag your 3D model anywhere on the canvas.

➢ To resize, grab a corner handle with the Move tool and drag to make the model bigger or smaller.

➢ For rotation, click once on the model with the Rotate View tool and then drag around the canvas.

➢ Right-click the model and use the options to flip or rotate the horizontal or vertical axis.

➢ Use layers to stack multiple 3D objects and fine-tune their positions.

➢ Take time tweaking the placement until your 3D model integrates into your Photoshop project.

3D Layers Panel

Once you've imported a 3D object into your Photoshop document, you can use the 3D Layer tools to manipulate and customize the model.

To access these tools, make sure the 3D layer is selected, then open the 3D panel by going to **Window > 3D**.

In the 3D panel you'll find options to:

➢ Rotate, roll, drag, and slide the 3D object on any axis

➢ Scale the object bigger or smaller

➢ Adjust shadows and lighting

➢ Select various parts of a complex 3D model

➢ Customize render settings and textures

➢ Animate or create 3D movement

Moving 3D Models

One of Photoshop's most useful 3D features is the ability to freely move models around a 3D space and scene. Here are two ways to move objects in 3D:

Using the 3D Axis

➢ Select the Move tool and click on the center axis of the 3D model.

➤ Drag the object in any direction to move it around the 3D space.

➤ Hold Shift while dragging to move in perfectly straight lines along the axis.

Using the 3D Camera Tools

➤ Select the 3D Camera Rotation tool from the toolbar.

➤ Click and drag within the document to rotate the virtual camera around the scene.

➤ As you move the camera, the positioning of 3D objects will change in perspective.

➤ Use the Pan, Zoom, and Roll tools to move in any direction.

Rotating 3D Models

Rotating 3D models allows you to view and customize them from different angles. There are a few ways to rotate 3D objects:

➤ Click once on the object with the Rotate View tool, then drag around the canvas to rotate.

➢ Use the rotate options in the 3D panel, which include free drag and degree-based rotation on the X, Y, and Z axis.

➢ Click and drag on the axis handles that appear when you select the 3D object with the Move tool.

➢ Right-click the object and use the contextual menu options for flipping and rotating.

➢ Animate rotation for movement overtime on the timeline panel.

➢ Take advantage of 3D rotation to showcase your models from every possible viewpoint.

3D Tools

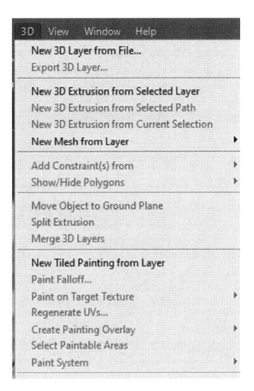

3D Material Tools

Materials in 3D graphics refer to the surface textures and properties that define how an object looks. Photoshop provides a robust set of material tools for customizing 3D models.

Here are some key material tools in Photoshop's 3D panel:

➤ Paint on textures directly onto the 3D model using the 3D Paint tools. Customize color, shine, bumps, and more.

➤ Apply preset materials like plastic, metal, wood, and fabric using the Materials menu.

➤ Adjust properties like reflection, shininess, bump, color, and many others using the Properties settings.

➤ Use the Material Editor to create custom materials and textures from scratch.

➤ Use image maps to map textures from 2D images onto your 3D models.

3D Camera Tools

Photoshop allows you to view and navigate around your 3D scene using a virtual camera. You can think of it as positioning an actual camera to photograph the objects.

Here are the key 3D camera tools:

3D Camera Rotation - Orbit and rotate around a central point to frame your scene.

Pan - Move the camera horizontally side-to-side or up-and-down.

Zoom - Functions like a zoom lens to move the camera closer or farther away.

Roll - Rotate the camera on its axis as if rolling sideways.

Walk - Move the camera forward and backward through the scene.

Focal Length - Adjusts the camera's field of view from wide-angle to telephoto.

3D Post-Processing Tools

Once your 3D models are created, you can enhance them using Photoshop's suite of post-processing tools. These include:

Image-Based Lighting - Uses environment maps to realistically light models.

High Dynamic Range - Increases contrast and color depth for enhanced realism.

Depth of Field - Simulates realistic camera focus falloff. Blurs foreground/background.

Fog - Adds atmospheric fog that interacts with objects at varied depths.

Bokeh - Creates realistic out-of-focus bokeh texture based on camera settings.

Antialiasing - Smooth edges and contours to minimize jagged lines.

Combine these effects to take your rendered 3D visuals to the next level.

Textures

Textures add visual interest and realism to your designs. Whether you're creating natural scenes, abstract art, text effects, and more, custom textures can enhance your projects.

Applying Textures

Importing and adding pre-made textures to your artwork is a great way to get started with textures in Photoshop. Here are some tips:

- Download free texture image files from online sources like Adobe Stock or TextureKing. Look for textures like paper, paint, rock, fabric, etc.
- Open your document and the desired texture file. Copy the texture.
- Create a new layer in your document. Paste the texture to apply it.
- Scale the pasted texture using **Edit > Transform** tools so it covers the area you want.
- Set the texture layer blending mode to Multiply, Overlay, etc. to integrate it.
- Add a layer mask to selectively hide parts of the texture. Paint on the mask.
- Lower the texture layer's opacity to make it more subtle.

Editing Textures

For more control, you can edit and modify existing textures. Some editing techniques include:

➤ Adjust brightness, contrast, and saturation to change texture colors.

➤ Use Transform tools to scale, rotate, skew, or warp the texture.

➤ Cut out sections of the texture to reveal layers below.

➤ Apply filters like Motion Blur, Ocean Ripple, etc. to the texture.

➤ Clone parts of the texture with the Clone Stamp tool.

➤ Hand-paint on the texture layer with Brush tools at low opacity.

➤ Combine multiple textures using layer blending modes.

Creating Bump Maps

Bump maps add simulated depth and texture without altering the actual 3D shape of an object. Here's how to create one:

- ➢ Make a new Black and white image. Highlights and shadows define depth.
- ➢ Paint gray tones using Brush tools with textures selected.
- ➢ Invert the black and white values by going to **Image > Adjustments > Invert.**
- ➢ Save the bump map for later use.
- ➢ To apply, place the object and bump map on layers. Set the map to Soft Light or Overlay blending.
- ➢ Adjust the bump map settings using **Filter > Filter Gallery > Texturizer** for customized effects.

Making Displacement Maps

Displacement maps physically move pixels to create sculpted 3D textures on an object. Steps:

- ➢ Follow the above steps to make a basic Black and white bump map.

- ➢ Expand the tonal range by applying Levels and Curve adjustments.

- ➢ Save the Displacement Map once you have strong black and white defined.

- ➢ To apply, select the object layer and go to **Filter > Displace**.

- ➢ Pick your map, set scaling, and click OK.

- ➢ Try modes like Stretch to Extremes for intense distortions.

Lights

Point Lights

Point lights simulate bulbs or focused light sources emitting light in a single direction. They create directional shadows and highlights. To use:

- ➢ Go to the 3D panel and click **"Create a New Light"** then choose Point Light.

➢ Adjust settings like color, intensity, and falloff distance in the Properties panel.

➢ Move the light around with the 3D Axis to angle it.

➢ Add multiple point lights together for complex setups.

➢ Use shadow options to enable/disable shadows.

Spot Lights

Spot lights cast focused cones of light in a specific direction, similar to a flashlight or spotlight. To create one:

➢ Create a new light and select Spot Light from the options.

➢ Adjust the spread angle, blend, intensity, color, and other properties.

➢ Rotate the light cone using the axis or numeric directional inputs.

➢ Layer multiple spot lights at different angles as needed.

➢ Enable shadows for visible beams and contrast.

➢ Take advantage of spot lights' directional precision to highlight objects or create moody scenes.

Infinite Lights

Infinite lights simulate natural light coming evenly from a distant source, like the sun. They produce soft shadows and shading. To use:

➢ Create a new light and choose Infinite Light from the menu.

➢ Set the elevation and altitude angles with the axis or numeric inputs.

➢ Adjust intensity, color, and shadow parameters as desired.

➢ Use multiple infinite lights together to blend several light directions.

➢ Rotate models instead of lights to adjust directional shading.

➢ Mimic real-world outdoor lighting by leveraging infinite lights from multiple angles.

Image-Based Lights

- ➤ For the most realistic lighting, use image-based lights, which sample the lighting properties from a photo.
- ➤ Select New Image Based Light and pick an HDRI lighting environment image.
- ➤ Set the image sampling intensity in the Properties panel.
- ➤ Rotate your model within the fixed image environment.
- ➤ Add extra lights as needed to get your ideal lighting balance.

Rendering

Rendering refers to the process of generating a 2D image from a 3D model using various lighting, texture, and camera effects. Photoshop 2024 offers three main rendering engines: Default, Ray Traced, and OpenGL.

Default Render

The Default render is Photoshop's standard production renderer. It's a good balance of speed and quality for basic 3D work. To use it:

> ➢ With your 3D model set up, go to **3D > Render**.
>
> ➢ Choose **"Default Render"** from the dialog box menu.
>
> ➢ Adjust settings like quality, lighting, and camera angle.
>
> ➢ Click Render to generate the image.
>
> ➢ Defaults render quickly with good color and lighting.
>
> ➢ Great for draft renders before final output.
>
> ➢ Take advantage of Default renders during the initial stages of 3D projects to preview models.

Ray Traced Render

For optimal realism with accurate light behavior, use Photoshop's Ray-Traced render engine. Steps:

> ➢ Go to **3D > Render** and select **"Ray Traced"** as the render engine.

- Set the **Image Quality** to **High** for best results.

- Adjust the Reflections, Refraction, and Shadows values.

- Enable options like diffuse textures and anti-aliasing.

- Render the image - this will take more time to calculate lighting.

- Ray Traced renders produce photorealistic output, perfect for final 3D images.

OpenGL Render

The OpenGL renderer uses graphics card hardware for enhanced performance and speed. To use:

- Go to **3D > Render** and choose **"OpenGL"** from the dropdown menu.

- Tweak settings like texture quality, shadows, and lighting.

- Check **Enable Textures** and **Enable Lighting** for best results.

- Set the output size and camera angle as desired.

➢ Click Render - OpenGL is very fast compared to other modes.

➢ OpenGL is ideal for quick draft renders and making rapid design iterations.

Video Layers

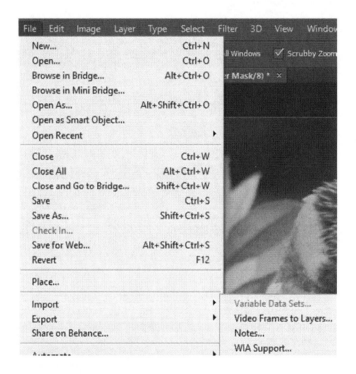

Importing Video

The first step is to import your video file into Photoshop. Here's how:

➢ Open Photoshop and create a new blank document. The size doesn't matter for now.

➢ Go to **File > Import** and choose your video file. Almost all common video formats are supported, including MP4, MOV, and AVI.

➢ A video layer will be created in your Layers panel. You'll see a thumbnail of the first frame.

➢ Once imported, you can make edits to the video layer just like any other layer in Photoshop. Now let's look at trimming the clip.

Trimming Clips

You may not want to use the whole video clip in your project. Photoshop makes it easy to trim the start and end points:

➢ In the Layers panel, double-click on the video layer thumbnail. This will open the video in its window.

➢ Move the playhead to the new start point and click the Set Start Time button (left bracket icon).

- Move the playhead to the new endpoint and click the Set End Time button (right bracket icon).
- Close the video window. Your clip will now play only the trimmed section.
- Trimming the clip will not delete any video footage - it only sets new in and out points. You can always reopen the clip and reset the start/end points.

Opacity/Blending

Photoshop has powerful tools for blending video with other layers:

- Reduce the Opacity of the video layer to make the content underneath show through.
- Try different Blending Modes like Screen, Multiply, or Overlay to dramatically change the video's interaction with the layers below.
- Add a Layer Mask to selectively hide portions of the video layer. Paint the mask with black/white to reveal/hide areas.

➢ Use Layer Styles like Drop Shadow or Glow to make the video pop.

➢ Blending modes create unique visual effects with just a few clicks.

Transforming Clips

Photoshop provides many ways to transform or distort your video clips:

➢ Use the Free Transform command (Ctrl/Cmd + T) to scale, rotate, or skew the clip. Right-click to access advanced options like Warp and Distort.

➢ Choose **Edit > Transform** to access individual transforms like Scale and Rotate.

➢ Click on the layer effects icon at the bottom of the Layers panel to find controls for Perspective and 3D transforms.

➢ Use the Puppet Warp tool to bend and shape parts of the video layer.

➢ Apply the Liquify filter to melt, expand, and shift the video in creative ways.

➢ Feel free to combine transforms for interesting effects. Just remember all transformations decrease video quality, so avoid overdoing it.

Animating Layers

To take your video layers to the next level, animate them over time:

➢ Click on the stopwatch icon next to the layer property you want to animate. This could be Position, Opacity, Styles, etc.

➢ Move the playhead to a new spot in the timeline. Adjust that layer property. A keyframe will be automatically added.

➢ Repeat moving the playhead and changing the property to create an animation path.

➢ For more control, right-click on layer keyframes to access options like easing and smoothing. The Animation panel also provides advanced tools.

Some examples of fun video animations:

➢ Animate position to make the video clip move across the frame.

➢ Fade opacity in or out to make the clip appear and disappear.

➢ Animate layer styles like Drop Shadow Size or Color.

➢ Use position keyframes and clipping masks together to selectively reveal parts of the video over time.

➢ Apply your creativity to bring your video compositions to life.

Timeline Panel

To access the timeline panel, open a Photoshop document with a video layer, then go to **Window > Timeline**. The timeline displays your video frames sequentially and allows you to add keyframes and other adjustments. Here's a quick overview of the timeline components:

Playhead - Indicates the current frame position. Scrub to navigate frames.

Zoom - Magnifies the timeline to view more or fewer frames.

Pan - Slides the visible timeline area sideways.

Now let's look at adding keyframes, the basis for animation.

Adding Keyframes

Keyframes mark specific properties like position or opacity at certain points in time:

1. Select the video layer to animate in the Layers panel.
2. On the timeline, move the playhead to where you want the first keyframe.
3. Click the stopwatch icon next to the property you want to animate. A keyframe appears.
4. Scrub the playhead to a new spot. Adjust that property in the Layers panel. Another keyframe appears.

5. Repeat steps 3-4 to create an animation path.

The timeline displays the property's keyframes and changes over time. Let's discover ways to fine-tune the animation.

Animation Options

Right-click on a keyframe for options like temporal interpolation, holding keyframes in place, and more:

➢ Easy Ease smooths the transition between keyframes.

➢ Rove Across Time lets keyframes move independently of each other.

➢ Convert to/from Hold Keyframes to maintain a property value.

➢ The timeline's Graph Editor provides further ways to adjust animation curves and velocity.

Tweens and Transitions

Create automatic changes between keyframes with tweens and transitions:

> - **Motion Tween** - Automatically interpolates position keyframes for smooth motion.
> - **Opacity Tween** - Transitions opacity between 0-100% keyframes.
> - Add transitions like **Cross Dissolve** to gradually fade video clips into each other.
> - Tweens ensure smooth and consistent changes over time, saving tedious manual animation work.

Effects and Presets

Enhance your video with built-in effects:

> - Click the Effects tab above the timeline.
> - Drag an effect like Color Balance onto the video layer.
> - Adjust effect parameters in the timeline or Layers panel.

➢ The Effects and Presets panels provide a huge range of options, from color correction to distortion effects. Try combining multiple effects for unique results.

➢ The timeline also allows you to customize and save effect presets for reuse.

Exporting Video

You've finished creating your awesome video project in Photoshop. Now it's time to export it as a video file you can share or use in other apps.

Render Video

Start by rendering your composite video in the Render Queue:

➢ Go to **File > Export > Render Video**. This adds your active composition to the queue.

➢ Click the Render button to process all layers, effects, and transforms into a preliminary video file.

➢ Rendering can take some time depending on length and complexity. Once done, you're ready to finalize the export settings.

Export Settings

In the Render Queue window, click on the underlined name of your render item to open export settings:

➢ Set your desired Frame Size like 720p or 1080p. Match the composition dimensions.

➢ Choose the playback Frame Rate - typically 24, 25, or 30 fps.

➢ Pick a suitable Duration or use In/Out points to trim length.

➢ Adjust settings to meet your project needs before exporting. Now let's pick an encoding format.

Encoding Options

Encoding determines compression and file format:

H.264 - High-quality MP4 videos. Balance of size and quality.

H.265 - Smaller HEVC files. Good for 4K. Requires compatible player.

Animation - Lossless but large file sizes.

ProRes - High quality but large QuickTime MOVs for post-production.

Try different encodings to find the ideal compression and quality for your needs.

Output Module

Finally, set where to export the video in the Output Module:

> ➢ Click on Output Module to open settings.
> ➢ Choose a filename and location to export to.
> ➢ Enable "Export As..." for formats like MP4, MOV, and AVI.
> ➢ Click Export to complete the process.
> ➢ Your rendered video will be saved as a standalone file you can now share or use in other video projects.

CHAPTER FIFTEEN

Opening Images in Camera Raw

Opening images in Camera Raw allows you to edit raw files and make non-destructive adjustments before opening them in Photoshop. Camera Raw gives you more flexibility and control when editing images compared to opening JPEGs or TIFFs directly in Photoshop.

Raw File Formats

Raw image files contain uncompressed, unprocessed data directly from your camera's sensor. Some common raw formats include:

.CR2 - Canon raw files

.NEF - Nikon raw files

.ARW - Sony raw files

.RW2 - Panasonic raw files

Raw files need to be processed to produce a viewable image, either in your camera when you take the photo or in editing software like Camera Raw. The main benefits of shooting in raw vs JPEG are:

➢ More flexibility for editing exposure, white balance, colors, etc.

➢ Higher image quality and less data loss

➢ Ability to recover more detail from highlights and shadows

➢ No image degradation from compression

Opening JPEGs and TIFFs in Camera Raw

While Camera Raw is designed for processing raw files, you can also open JPEG and TIFF files. Here's how:

➢ In Photoshop, go to **File > Open**

➢ Select the JPEG or TIFF file you want to open

➢ Check the box for **'Open as Smart Object'**

➢ Click OK

This will open the file in Camera Raw as a smart object with the raw processing controls. While you won't have quite as much flexibility as a true raw file, you'll have more editing options than opening the JPEG directly in Photoshop.

Opening Images in Camera Raw from Bridge

Adobe Bridge is a useful file browser and organizer for creative workflows. Here are the steps to open photos in Camera Raw from Bridge:

> ➢ Launch Adobe Bridge from within Photoshop under **File > Browse in Bridge.**
> ➢ Navigate to the folder containing your image files.
> ➢ Select the photo you want to open in Camera Raw. You can select multiple images to open at once.

➢ Right-click on the selected images and choose **"Open in Camera Raw"** from the menu.

➢ The images will launch directly into the Camera Raw workspace.

➢ After making any edits, click **"Open Image"** to open as layers in Photoshop.

Opening Images in Camera Raw from Photoshop

You can also access Camera Raw directly from within the Photoshop workspace:

➢ In Photoshop, go to **File > Open**

➢ Select the raw file you want to open. If opening a JPEG or TIFF, make sure **"Open as Smart Object"** is checked.

➢ Click Open.

➢ The image will launch in the Camera Raw dialog box rather than opening directly in Photoshop.

➢ From here, you can start processing your raw image files or JPEGs/TIFFs in Camera Raw.

Interface and Tools

When you open a raw file or JPEG/TIFF in Camera Raw from Photoshop or Adobe Bridge, you'll see the image in the preview area with various tools on the right.

Zooming, Panning, and Rotating

Before you start editing, you'll want to zoom in and inspect areas of the image and rotate if needed:

➢ **Zoom -** Click the Zoom tool, then click on the image to zoom in. Alt/Option + click to zoom out.

> **Pan -** With the Zoom tool selected, click and drag on the image to move around the preview.

> **Rotate -** Click on the Rotate Crop Frame tool and use the angle slider to rotate the image.

> **Reset -** To undo zooming and rotation, click on the small Reset Crop Frame icon.

Adjusting White Balance

One of the most important Camera Raw edits is adjusting the white balance to neutralize color casts:

> In the Basic panel, click on the White Balance Selector tool.

> Click on an area in the image that should be neutral white/gray.

> The temperature and tint will automatically adjust.

> You can also manually adjust the Temp and Tint sliders for finer tweaks.

Using the Crop Tool

Cropping in Camera Raw is non-destructive, allowing you to change the crop later:

➤ Select the Crop tool. Click and drag the edges or corners of the crop border.

➤ Adjust the aspect ratio with the selections at the top of the toolbar.

➤ Click the Clear Cropping box to undo the crop.

➤ When ready, click Open Image to apply the crop.

Using the Adjustment Brush

The Adjustment Brush lets you selectively edit specific parts of the image:

➤ Select the Adjustment Brush tool (or press K).

➤ Set exposure, clarity, or other effects using the sliders.

- ➢ Paint over the area you want to adjust with the brush.
- ➢ Fine-tune the brush stroke with the Erase, Feather, and Flow options.
- ➢ Create multiple adjustment layers using the New radio button.
- ➢ The Adjustment Brush is ideal for enhancing eyes, saturating colors, or brightening parts of the image.

Applying Presets

Use presets to quickly get consistent results for your photos:

- ➢ Click on Presets in the toolbar to open the preset panel.
- ➢ Click on a category folder, then hover over the presets to preview your image.
- ➢ Click on the preset you want to apply.
- ➢ Adjust the Amount slider to control the preset intensity.
- ➢ Save new presets of your edits by clicking the + icon in the Presets panel.

Basic Adjustments

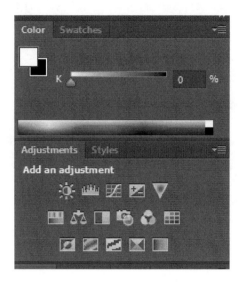

The Basic panel is the first place to start when processing raw images in Camera Raw.

These sliders give precise control over the core corrections needed to take your photos from flat to phenomenal.

Adjusting White Balance

White balance controls the overall color tone. Fix color casts by:

➢ Using the White Balance Tool - Click on a neutral white/gray area.

➢ Temp/Tint Sliders - Manually correct color casts.

➢ Auto - Applies automatic white balance correction.

➢ Neutralizing white balance should generally be the first edit.

Optimizing Exposure

The Exposure slider brightens or darkens your entire image. To properly expose:

➢ Check the histogram - Adjust exposure to center the histogram.

➢ Highlight clipping - Reduce exposure if highlights are blown out.

➢ Shadow clipping - Increase exposure to reveal more shadows.

➢ Compensate for difficult lighting.

➢ Use Exposure judiciously to avoid degrading image quality.

Adding Contrast

> ➤ The Contrast slider increases or decreases the separation between the darkest and lightest areas.

> ➤ Increase contrast moderately for more vivid images.

> ➤ Be careful not to overdo it causing clipped shadows/highlights.

> ➤ Decrease contrast for flatter, muted images.

> ➤ Contrast works hand-in-hand with clarity and vibrance for balanced results.

Enhancing Highlights and Shadows

> ➤ The Highlights and Shadows sliders target the bright and dark regions, respectively.

> ➤ Drag Highlights left to recover overexposed, clipped highlights.

> ➤ Drag Shadows right to brighten underexposed, clipped shadows.

> ➤ Take care not to go too far causing image degradation or an unnatural HDR look.

Adding Clarity

- ➤ The Clarity slider increases mid-tone contrast to add "punch" and apparent sharpness.
- ➤ Increase Clarity moderately for more vivid images.
- ➤ Too much Clarity can cause unrealistic halos at the edges.
- ➤ Decrease Clarity for softened, dream-like effects.
- ➤ Start at a low setting and slowly increase Clarity to enhance image pop.

Boosting Vibrance and Saturation

- ➤ Vibrance intelligently saturates colors without overdoing skin tones. Saturation affects all colors equally.
- ➤ Increase Vibrance moderately for nice color enhancement.
- ➤ Only increase Saturation slightly to avoid oversaturated colors.

➤ Decrease both for muted, vintage effects.

➤ Vibrance should be your primary color intensity tool, with Saturation used sparingly.

Tone Curve

The Tone Curve graphs the tonal range of your image, from dark shadows to bright highlights. Adjustments made to the curve apply contrast and color shifts in specific tonal regions.

Using the Point Curve

The Point Curve lets you adjust specific points on the curve:

➤ Click on the Point tab.

➤ Add points by clicking on the curve line.

➤ Drag points up/down to adjust contrast and tone.

➤ The lower right brightens highlights, upper left darkens shadows.

➤ Use the Point curve for precise contrast enhancements to specific tonal ranges.

Using the Region Curve

The Region curve divides the image into highlight, lightness, darkness, and shadow regions:

➤ Click on the Region tab.

➤ Use the sliders to target adjustments:

➤ **Highlights** - Adjust the right of the first slider

➤ **Lights** - Between the first two sliders

➤ **Darks** - Between the last two sliders

➤ **Shadows** - Adjust the left of the last slider

➤ The Region sliders provide an intuitive way to adjust contrast and color in tonal zones.

Applying Tone Curve Presets

Camera Raw includes many creative tone curve presets to experiment with:

➤ Click on the Presets tab.

➢ Click on a preset folder, then a preset thumbnail.

➢ Adjust the Amount slider to control the preset intensity.

➢ Try Medium Contrast, Strong Contrast, and different color-grading presets.

Inverting the Tone Curve

Inverting the curve creates a color-negative effect:

➢ In the Point or Region curve, click on the double-arrow icon to invert.

➢ Adjust the curve or sliders.

➢ Click the icon again to revert to the original curve.

➢ Inverting can produce interesting high-contrast, color-inverted versions of your image.

HSL/Grayscale

HSL stands for:

Hue - The color itself

Saturation - The color vibrancy

Luminance - The color brightness

The HSL/Grayscale panel lets you adjust each of these properties for individual colors and color ranges. For example, you can:

➤ Boost the greens in a landscape

➤ Mute overly saturated reds in a photo

➤ Brighten the blues in a portrait

➤ And more for refined color control

Adjusting Hue

To shift color hues:

➤ Click on the HSL/Color/B&W tab.

➤ Go to the Hue panel.

➤ Drag the color sliders left/right to alter hues.

➤ Small hue adjustments can correct color casts or change color schemes.

Enhancing Saturation

To alter color saturation:

➤ Switch to the Saturation panel.

➤ Drag sliders right to saturate, left to desaturate.

➤ Be careful not to oversaturate causing an unnatural effect.

➤ Targeted saturation tweaks make certain colors pop while muting others.

Modifying Luminance

To lighten/darken specific hues:

➤ Switch to the Luminance panel.

➤ Drag sliders right to lighten, left to darken.

➤ Luminance edits define subjects against backgrounds.

➤ For example, lightening skin tones against a darkened background.

Making Targeted Adjustments

For more precise color changes:

➢ Select the Targeted Adjustment Tool (TAT).

➢ Click-drag left/right over a color in the image.

➢ This adjusts hues, saturation, and luminance together.

➢ The TAT lets you easily enhance colors in specific image regions.

Converting to Black & White

To convert to grayscale:

➢ At the top of the panel, click B&W.

➢ Adjust the color sliders to sculpt blacks, whites, and grays.

➢ Toggle between color and B&W to compare.

➢ Use HSL as a flexible black-and-white conversion tool.

Split Toning

Unlike traditional color filters, split toning gives you advanced creative control when color-grading your images.

Choosing a Highlight Color

To pick a highlight tint:

- ➢ In the Split Toning panel, click on Highlights.
- ➢ Click on the color square to open the picker.
- ➢ Select a hue to tint the highlights.
- ➢ Choose warm tones like yellow/orange to enhance sunsets or skin. Cool tones like blue/purple work well for night scenes.

Choosing a Shadow Color

To pick a shadow tint:

- ➢ Click on Shadows.
- ➢ Open the color picker.
- ➢ Choose a hue to tint the shadows.
- ➢ Often a complementary color to the highlights looks best. Browns and olive greens also work well in shadows.

Adjusting the Balance

The Balance slider controls the strength of the highlights vs. shadows:

➢ Slide right to emphasize the highlight color.

➢ Slide left to emphasize the shadow color.

➢ Split the difference for an even split-tone effect.

Controlling the Application

Use these options to refine where the tones are applied:

➢ **Saturation -** Controls the saturation intensity of the colors.

➢ **Highlights** - Limits split toning to mostly highlights.

➢ **Shadows** - Limits split toning to mostly shadows.

Simulating a Duotone Effect

To create a stylized black-and-white duotone:

➢ Convert to grayscale in the HSL/Color panel.

➢ Use split toning to add one hue to shadows, and another to highlights.

➢ Adjust the Balance and Application sliders.

Detail

The Detail panel provides important sharpening and noise reduction controls for processing your raw images.

Adjusting Sharpening

To sharpen crisply without artifacts:

- ➢ Hold the Alt/Option key while dragging the Amount slider to preview where sharpening is applied.
- ➢ Increase the Radius to sharpen larger edges.
- ➢ Reduce Detail to control halos and artifacts.
- ➢ Masking sharpens edges but not smooth areas like skies.
- ➢ Sharpen moderately - too much looks unnatural. Zoom to 100% to inspect the results.

Reducing Luminance Noise

To minimize grainy noise:

- ➢ Zoom to 100% to view noise.

➢ Increase the Luminance slider until the noise is sufficiently reduced.

➢ Hold Alt/Option while adjusting Luminance to preview where noise is reduced.

➢ Balance Luminance with Sharpening to avoid over-softening.

➢ Luminance works well for moderate noise but struggles with heavy noise.

Eliminating Color Noise

To remove splotchy color noise:

➢ Zoom to 100% to inspect color noise.

➢ Increase the Color slider until color speckles are smoothed out.

➢ Hold down Alt/Option to preview where color noise is reduced.

➢ Remove color noise without sacrificing color details.

➢ For best results, apply Color noise reduction separately from Luminance.

Using Noise Reduction First

An effective sharpening workflow is:

> ➢ First, reduce noise with Luminance and Color.
> ➢ Then increase Sharpening to bring back crispness.
> ➢ Finish by fine-tuning Sharpening Masking and Detail.
> ➢ Noise reduction first allows you to sharpen cleanly and selectively.

Lens Corrections

The Lens Corrections panel lets you fix common lens flaws like distortion, vignetting, and chromatic aberration. Correcting these issues makes your photos sharper and less distorted. The fixes are non-destructive when using Camera Raw.

Applying Profile Corrections

To automatically fix lens flaws:

> ➢ In the Lens Corrections panel, check Enable Profile Corrections.
>
> ➢ Select your Camera Make, Camera Model, and Lens Profile.
>
> ➢ Check Remove Chromatic Aberration and Enable Defringe.
>
> ➢ Toggle corrections on/off to compare the before/after.
>
> ➢ Lens profiles apply preset corrections optimized for your specific gear.

Using the Manual Transform Tools

For further tweaking:

> ➢ Adjust Distortion to straighten barrel/pincushion warping.
>
> ➢ Use the Vertical/Horizontal/Rotate tools to level the horizon and straighten.
>
> ➢ Check Constrain Crop to avoid unfilled edges.

➢ Manual adjustments give you flexibility beyond the lens profile corrections.

Reducing Chromatic Aberration

To minimize color fringing:

➢ Zoom to 100% to view color fringing clearly.

➢ Enable the Defringe and increase the Purple Amount/Green Amount to neutralize fringing.

➢ Check Show Edges to preview the affected area.

➢ Defringing removes distracting color artifacts along high-contrast edges.

Correcting Vignetting

To fix darkened corners:

➢ Increase the Amount slider to lighten vignetting.

➢ Adjust the Midpoint to control the strength of the correction.

➢ Fixing vignetting gives your image a more consistent exposure across the frame.

Camera Calibration

The Camera Calibration panel provides powerful creative color grading tools. You can change primary hues, adjust HSL sliders per channel, and apply shadow and highlight tinting.

Adjusting the Primary RGB Hues

To alter the red, green, and blue primaries:

- ➢ In the Camera Calibration panel, adjust the Red, Green, and Blue Hue sliders.
- ➢ Make small adjustments to the primary hues. Dramatic shifts look unnatural.
- ➢ Red/Yellow changes skin tone, Green foliage, Blue skies.

Using the HSL Sliders

- ➢ To separately control Hue, Saturation, and Luminance per channel:
- ➢ Click on the Red, Green, or Blue tab.

➢ Adjust the Hue, Saturation, and Luminance sliders.

➢ Target specific color properties in the red, green, and blue channels.

Applying a Shadow Tint

To color grade the shadows:

➢ Switch to the Shadows tab.

➢ Click on the color square to open the picker.

➢ Choose a hue to subtly tint the shadows.

➢ Try subtle blue, green, or purple shadow tints.

Applying a Highlight Tint

To color grade the highlights:

➢ Switch to the Highlights tab.

➢ Click the color square and pick a highlight hue.

➢ Warm tones like orange and yellow work well in highlights.

Using Camera Calibration Presets

For creative color effects:

- ➢ Click on the Presets tab.
- ➢ Click on a preset thumbnail to apply.
- ➢ Adjust the Amount slider to control the intensity.
- ➢ Vintage, cinematic, and black-and-white presets are provided.

Saving and Exporting

After processing your photos in Camera Raw, you'll need to save the changes and open or export the images in Photoshop. Camera Raw provides flexible options for saving your work as PSDs, JPEGs, TIFFs, or DNGs.

Using the Save Image Button

To save adjustments without changing pixels:

- ➢ Adjust your image in Camera Raw.

➢ Click on the Save Image button or press Ctrl/Cmd + S.

➢ Camera Raw saves your settings in the XMP sidecar file.

➢ When reopened, settings will be reapplied non-destructively.

➢ Save Image should be used regularly to back up work in progress.

Opening Images in Photoshop

To apply edits and further process:

➢ Adjust the image in Camera Raw.

➢ Click Open Image or press Ctrl/Cmd + O.

➢ Choose options like PSD, smart object, and color space.

➢ The image will open as a layer or smart object in Photoshop.

➢ Open when ready to transition from raw processing to compositing.

Exporting JPEGs from Camera Raw

To save high-quality JPEGs:

> ➤ Adjust images in Camera Raw.
>
> ➤ Click the Export button.
>
> ➤ Select JPEG as the file format.
>
> ➤ Adjust quality, size, and sharpening.
>
> ➤ Select a folder to save the JPEG exports.

Exporting TIFFs from Camera Raw

To save uncompressed TIFFs:

> ➤ Follow the JPEG steps but select TIFF in the export dialog.
>
> ➤ TIFFs retain all image data at a large file size.
>
> ➤ Use TIFFs for high-resolution printing or archiving edited RAWs.

Converting Images to DNG

To create archival DNG raw files:

➢ In the export dialog, choose DNG as the file format.

➢ DNG converts proprietary RAWs into an open-source DNG raw format.

➢ Use DNG for backing up adjusted raw files or archiving.

CHAPTER SIXTEEN

Channel Basics

Channels are an important yet often overlooked feature that allow you to view different color components of an image separately, make color adjustments, create masks, and more.

RGB Channels

The default mode for new Photoshop files is RGB color. This stands for red, green, and blue - the three primary colors used for displaying images on screen. In RGB mode, an image will have the following channels:

Red Channel - Shows the intensity of red in the image

Green Channel - Shows the intensity of green

Blue Channel - Shows the intensity of blue

When viewing these channels individually in the Channels panel, you will see a grayscale version of the image based on that color intensity. The brighter areas indicate more presence of that color channel.

To view the individual RGB channels:

➢ Open an image and ensure the working space is RGB Color.
➢ Click **Window > Channels** to open the Channels panel.
➢ Click on each channel name to view just that channel.

Use RGB channels to evaluate the intensity of certain colors or to make color adjustments. For example, add contrast to just the blue channel to emphasize blue tones.

CMYK Channels

CMYK stands for cyan, magenta, yellow, and key (black). This four-color process is used for color printing.

When converting an RGB image to CMYK color mode, Photoshop will generate the following CMYK channels:

- ➢ **Cyan -** Shows the intensity of cyan ink
- ➢ **Magenta -** Shows the intensity of magenta ink
- ➢ **Yellow -** Shows the intensity of yellow ink
- ➢ **Black -** Shows the intensity of black ink

To view CMYK channels:

- ➢ Convert the image to CMYK Color mode (**Image > Mode > CMYK Color**).
- ➢ Open the Channels panel.
- ➢ Click on each CMYK channel name to view it.

➤ Evaluating your CMYK channels helps catch any unwanted ink overlap and anticipate how colors will print. Make adjustments to the channels to solve printing issues.

Alpha Channels

Alpha channels contain transparency information - they define areas of the image that should be transparent or semi-transparent rather than solid colors. Photoshop automatically generates an Alpha 1 channel when certain tools like selection tools are used.

To view alpha channels:

➤ Click **Window > Channels.**
➤ Scroll down past the color channels to see any alpha channels.
➤ The grayscale visualizes the transparency, with solid black areas being 100% transparent. Alpha channels let you save and load selections as well as create masks.

How to Create an Alpha Channel

- ➢ Make a selection with any selection tool.
- ➢ At the bottom of the Channels panel, click Save Selection as Channel.
- ➢ Name the channel and click OK.
- ➢ This will store the selection as a new alpha channel that can be viewed and edited like other channels.

Using the Channels Panel

The Channels panel displays all the channels for an image in one place. Here are some key features:

View channels - Click the eye icon to show/hide a channel.

Select channels - Ctrl/Cmd-click multiple channels to select them.

Add color - Double-click a spot on a channel to assign color.

Blend channels - Drag a channel into another to blend them.

Duplicate channels - Drag a channel onto the new channel icon.

Delete channels - Drag a channel onto the trash icon.

The Channel panel toolbar also includes options for splitting and merging channels.

Selecting Channels

Selecting channels allows you to isolate specific color and tonal information in an image. Once selected, channels can be adjusted, used for masks, or loaded as selections.

Viewing Individual Channels

To select and view a single channel:

➤ Open an image and click **Window > Channels** to open the Channels panel.

Click on the channel name to view that channel individually:

➢ RGB has Red, Green, and Blue channels

➢ CMYK has Cyan, Magenta, Yellow, and Black channels

➢ Click RGB/CMYK to view the composite channel

➢ The channel will display as a grayscale image based on the channel information.

➢ Adjust the viewed channel as needed using commands like Levels and Curves.

➢ To return to the full-color image, click the RGB/CMYK composite channel.

Selecting Multiple Channels

To select two or more channels in the Channels panel:

➢ Make sure the Channels panel is visible.

➢ Hold Ctrl (Win)/Command (Mac) and click to select multiple channels.

➢ Selected channels will be highlighted.

➢ You can now adjust only the selected channels.

➢ Ctrl/Command-click again on selected channels to deselect them.

➢ This technique is useful for swapping color channels or making adjustments to a specific color range.

Loading a Channel as a Selection

Channel information can be loaded as a selection:

➢ In the Channels panel, select the channel to load.

➢ Click the Load channel as a selection icon at the bottom of the panel.

➢ The active channel will be loaded as a selection on the image.

➢ Use this selection to isolate and edit specific parts of the image.

➢ To save the selection, click Save Selection as Channel.

Creating Alpha Channels

Alpha channels are grayscale masks that store selection information in Photoshop. They allow you to save a selection so it can be modified and reused in the future.

Creating an Alpha Channel from a

Selection

Make a selection using any of the Photoshop 2024 selection tools. This can include:

➢ Marquee tools for rectangular/elliptical selections
➢ Lasso tools for freeform selections
➢ The Magic Wand to select based on tone and color

➢ The Quick Selection for fast, intelligent selection

➢ Go to the **Channels** panel and click **Save Selection as Channel** at the bottom.

➢ In the dialog box, name your alpha channel and click OK.

➢ The selection will be stored as a new alpha channel visible in the Channels panel.

➢ You can now load and modify this channel anytime as a selection.

Tips:

➢ Adjust selection edges before saving for best results.

➢ Name channels clearly to organize and identify them.

➢ Click the eye icon to show/hide the channel overlay.

➢ Creating an Alpha Channel from Transparency

➢ On your base image layer, add transparency through means like masking or erasing.

➢ Go to the Channels panel and click Save Transparency as Channel.

➢ Name the new alpha channel and click OK.

➢ The transparent areas will be stored as a channel that can be loaded as a selection or mask.

➢ Adjust the channel values to modify the transparent effect.

Pro tips:

➢ Use brush tools with soft edges to create natural transparency.

➢ Use Lock Transparent Pixels on a layer to maintain transparency.

➢ Invert the channel to reverse the transparency.

Modifying Alpha Channels

Once created, alpha channels can be edited to update the selection/transparency:

➢ Levels and Curves can adjust channel tonality

➢ Blur filters can soften channel edges

➢ The Paintbrush can directly paint channel opacity

➢ Inverting the channel reverses the mask

Channel Mixer

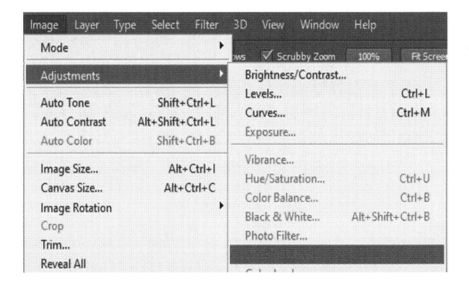

The Channel Mixer is a powerful adjustment tool for changing colors and tones in an image by mixing color channels.

Mixing Color Channels

The Channel Mixer lets you take a source channel like a red, green, or blue channel and mix it with other channels to alter color and contrast.

To mix channels:

➢ Go to **Image > Adjustments > Channel Mixer**.

➢ Below each output channel, adjust the source channel sliders.

For example:

➢ Boost the Red slider for the Red output channel.

➢ Increase the Blue slider for the Green output.

➢ Watch the image change as you mix the channels.

➢ Adjust the sliders until you achieve the desired effect.

➢ Click OK to apply the channel mixing.

Tips:

➢ Keep outputs at 100% or colors will be muted.

➢ Try subtle mixing for naturalistic corrections.

➢ Mix opposite colors for more dramatic effects.

Monochrome Conversion

The Channel Mixer provides an excellent tool for black-and-white conversion:

➢ Go to **Image > Adjustments > Channel Mixer**.

➢ Set the Red, Green, and Blue output channels each to:

➢ **Red Source:** 30%

➢ **Green Source:** 59%

➢ **Blue Source:** 11%

➢ Click OK to convert to monochrome.

➢ Adjust source sliders to fine-tune the black-and-white effect.

➢ This mixes the channels into a detailed grayscale image perfect for monochrome photography.

Custom Black and White

For more control over monochrome conversion:

➢ Select **Image > Adjustments > Black & White**.

➢ Click the Tint checkbox to enable channel mixing.

➢ Adjust the sliders below each color label to set custom mixing.

➢ Dragging a slider right will darken those original colors in black and white.

➢ Tweak the sliders until you achieve the desired tone and contrast.

➢ Re-adjust at any time to further customize the effect.

➢ Save your custom presets to quickly reapply your signature black-and-white looks.

Blending Channels

Blending channels allows you to combine multiple channels to produce creative effects and color alterations. By stacking and mixing channels, you can enhance specific colors, add visual interest, and generate artistic images.

Add Channels

To visually blend channels:

> ➢ Open an image and ensure the Channels panel is visible.
> ➢ Ctrl/Cmd-click to select the channels you want to blend.
> ➢ Click the Create New Channel icon at the bottom of the panel.
> ➢ Choose New Spot Channel.
> ➢ This will create a new channel composed of the blended selections.
> ➢ Adjust opacity to tweak the blend intensity.
> ➢ Blending spots of color is an easy way to make colors pop for vibrant images.

Maximum and Minimum

For more blend options:

> ➢ Select channels to blend as before.

- ➢ Right-click the channels and choose Blend Channels.
- ➢ Select Maximum or Minimum to blend by lightness.
- ➢ Maximum shows the lightest areas.
- ➢ The minimum shows the darkest areas.
- ➢ Blend modes like Multiply can also be used.
- ➢ Adjust layer opacity on the blended channel to fine-tune it.

Overlay Channels

To overlay channels for contrast effects:

- ➢ In the Channels panel, select a target channel to alter.
- ➢ Drag a source channel directly on top of the target channel.
- ➢ This will overlay the source channel based on blend mode.
- ➢ Repeat to stack multiple channels and intensify the effect.
- ➢ Reorder channels by dragging to change the blend interaction.

Subtract Channels

To subtract channels for precise blending:

➢ Select the two channels to blend in the panel.

➢ Right-click and choose Subtract Channels.

➢ The top channel will be subtracted from the bottom channel.

➢ Areas where channels overlap are removed for a precise effect.

Advanced Compositing

Compositing multiple images together can be taken to the next level using channels. It provides more control over selections, masks, and blending options for seamless composites.

Complex Channel Masks

Channel masks allow you to blend images with precision:

1. Add image layers you want to composite together.

2. Select a layer and click the Add Layer Mask icon at the bottom of the Layers panel.

3. Hold Ctrl/Cmd and click a channel in the Channels panel to load it as a selection.

4. The selection will become a layer mask on the selected layer.

5. Adjust mask density in the Properties panel for transparency mixing.

6. Repeat with other channels/layers to combine channel mask effects.

Pro tips:

➢ Use alpha channels as layer masks for intricate blending.

➢ Mask multiple layers with the same channel for consistency.

➢ Refine masks with Mask Feathering and Mask Edge.

Stacking Channels

Stacking channels together builds up a mask:

> ➤ Click the Create New Layer icon at the bottom of the Layers panel.
>
> ➤ Hold Ctrl/Cmd and click to load a channel as a selection on this layer.
>
> ➤ Choose Select > Modify > Contract to contract the selection by a few pixels.
>
> ➤ Fill the selection with black or white.
>
> ➤ Repeat with other channels, contracting each selection to stack the mask.
>
> ➤ Lower the Fill Opacity so the layers blend.
>
> ➤ This creates a smooth, customizable transition mask from the stacked channels.

Channel Arithmetic

To blend channels mathematically:

> ➤ Convert image layers to smart objects to preserve quality.
>
> ➤ Make both layers active by Shift-clicking them.

➢ Go to **Image > Apply Image**.

➢ Under Layer, choose the top layer source.

➢ Set Blending to an arithmetic operation like Subtract or Divide.

➢ This blends the source and target based on the math function.

➢ Adjust layer opacity or fill values to fine-tune the result.

CHAPTER SEVENTEEN

Creating Smart Objects

Smart objects are layers that contain image data from raster images or vector objects. The key benefit of smart objects is that they preserve an image's source content, allowing you to perform non-destructive edits.

Some advantages of using smart objects include:

Non-destructive transforms - You can freely scale, rotate, skew, or warp a smart object without damaging the original image.

Non-destructive filtering - Apply filters to smart objects non-destructively so you can go back and edit filters later.

Linked assets - If you update the source file for a smart object, the linked version also updates in Photoshop.

Flexible layer handling - Easily convert smart objects to layers or vice versa.

Understanding these will help you take full advantage of smart objects in your workflow.

Converting Layers to Smart Objects

Converting existing layers to smart objects is straightforward:

> ➤ In Photoshop 2024, open the document containing the layers you want to convert.

➤ In the Layers panel, select the layer(s) you wish to convert. To select multiple layers, hold Shift or Control (PC)/Command (Mac) while clicking.

➤ Right-click on a selected layer and choose "Convert to Smart Object." You can also go to Layer > Smart Objects > Convert to Smart Object.

➤ Each selected layer will be converted into its smart object layer in the Layers panel.

The selected layers are now enclosed within a smart object. You'll see a small icon appear at the lower right corner of the smart object thumbnails to indicate they are now smart objects.

Importing Files as Smart Objects

You can also import files directly as new smart objects:

➤ Proceed to File > Place Embedded.

➢ Browse to the file you wish to import. This can be a photo, RAW file, Illustrator artboard, PDF, or any other type of supported file.

➢ Select the file and click Place.

➢ Check the box for "Convert to Smart Object" and click OK.

➢ The file will be placed as a new smart object layer in your document.

➢ Alternatively, you can drag and drop a file right into an open Photoshop document to import it as a smart object. Just hold Shift while dragging to import it as a smart object rather than a regular layer.

Some tips for importing smart objects:

➢ Vector files like Illustrator artboards will remain scalable when imported as smart objects.

➢ You can import Camera RAW files as smart objects to apply non-destructive RAW edits.

➢ Imported smart objects are linked to their original files - so if the original changes, the content updates.

Transforming and Editing Smart Objects

Once set up, working with your smart objects is very straightforward:

Scale and transform freely - You can scale, rotate, skew, distort, or warp a smart object without damaging the original data.

Filter non-destructively - Apply filters like blurs, sharpening, distortions, etc. as smart filters that remain editable later.

Edit contents - Double-click a smart object thumbnail to open and edit the source image data (in either Photoshop or Illustrator). Save to update changes.

Export contents - Right-click a smart object and choose Export Contents to generate a separate file of the contents.

Replace contents - To replace the image or artwork within a smart object, right-click and select Replace Contents.

Convert back to layers - To finalize edits and convert a smart object to regular layers, right-click and select Rasterize.

Using these options, you can easily manipulate and experiment with smart objects while maintaining the flexibility to go back and edit the source data.

Smart Object Layer Masks

A layer mask hides or reveals portions of the content on a layer or smart object. Masks let you selectively blend layers and make localized adjustments. Applying masks to smart objects takes this to the next level for non-destructive editing.

Using Masks on Smart Objects

Adding a mask to a smart object layer is very straightforward:

➤ Select the smart object layer that needs a mask.

➤ Click the "Add layer mask" button at the bottom of the Layers panel. A plain white mask will be added.

➤ Use brush tools and black/white colors to paint on the mask and hide/reveal the smart object.

You can also:

➤ Add vector masks with Pen tools.

➤ Paste an existing mask onto a smart object.

➤ Load selections into masks to quickly mask areas.

➤ Painting with shades of gray will partially hide/reveal those areas. The mask remains non-destructively linked to the smart object.

Mask Alignment

By default, masks align to the edges of the smart object layer. To detach and move a mask independently:

➢ Right-click on the smart object layer.

➢ Choose "Enable Layer Mask Position".

➢ This will unlock the mask so you can reposition it. To realign, disable the mask position option.

Mask Density

To control mask opacity or density:

➢ Make sure the mask is selected in the Layers panel.

➢ Adjust the mask density slider at the top of the panel.

➢ Lower density fades the mask, increasing density strengthens it. Density affects how strongly the mask hides/reveals the smart object.

➢ You can also use Curves or Level adjustments to manipulate mask tones for precise density control.

Editing Masked Smart Objects

Once masked, you can selectively apply edits or filters within the masked area:

> ➢ Create a selection from the mask, then edit locally.
> ➢ Clip adjustment layers only affect the masked region.
> ➢ Paint filters or effects onto the mask.
> ➢ Double-click the masked smart object to edit its contents directly.
> ➢ Masking therefore allows sophisticated, non-destructive local adjustments and effects.

Linked Copies

One of the most useful features of smart objects in Photoshop is the ability to create linked copies that stay connected to the original smart object. This allows you to reuse the same content across multiple instances while maintaining a live link for seamless updates.

Duplicating a Smart Object

Creating linked copies is very straightforward:

➢ Select the smart object layer you want to duplicate.

➢ Press Command/Ctrl + J to duplicate the layer.

➢ In the Layers panel, Right-click the copy and choose "Convert to Linked."

➢ The copy will now display a chain link icon, indicating it is linked. Repeat this process to create multiple linked copies.

Updating from the Original Smart Object

When you edit and update the original smart object, those changes will ripple through to all linked copies:

➢ Double-click the original smart object thumbnail to open its contents.

➢ Edit the content document as needed, then save and close.

➢ Back in the main Photoshop file, all linked copies will be automatically updated to reflect your edits.

➢ This streamlines your workflow by allowing one-time edits that update across multiple copies.

Embedding vs Linking

If you want to break the link to a copy and embed its current contents:

➢ Select the linked copy layer in the Layers panel.

➢ Right-click and choose "Embed Linked" from the menu.

➢ This will embed the copy's current data state as its independent smart object, no longer linked to the original.

➢ You can reestablish links anytime by creating new linked duplicates. Keep in mind embedding large source files can bloat overall document size.

Managing Links

> ➢ To manage links and sources, go to Photoshop > File > Manage Links:
> ➢ View details on link statuses and sources.
> ➢ Update modified links.
> ➢ Replace a source by redirecting links.
> ➢ Break links to embed copies if needed.
> ➢ Actively monitoring and organizing links will ensure everything stays up to date within your documents.

Layer Comps

Layer comps allow you to capture different layer visibility states in your Photoshop document. When combined with smart objects, layer comps become a powerful way to manage variations and options for flexible re-editing.

Capturing Layer Comps

Here is a simple workflow for capturing layer comps:

➢ Set up your base layer stack, including any moveable or toggled layers.

➢ Make sure any layers you may toggle are smart objects.

➢ Click the "Create new Layer Comp" icon at the bottom of the Layers panel.

➢ Name and save the comp.

➢ Adjust toggled layers to new states and repeat capturing into additional named comps.

➢ Use the Layer Comps dropdown to quickly switch between your captured variations.

Loading Layer Comps

You can load a comp in one click to restore its layer visibility states:

➢ Select the layer comp you want to load from the Layer Comps dropdown.

➢ Click the "Load Layer Comp" icon near the bottom of the Layers panel.

➢ The visibility, position, and appearance of layers will be restored to match the selected comp.

➢ Make any needed changes, then re-capture an updated version of that comp.

➢ This allows smooth back-and-forth editing between different variations.

Layer Comps with Smart Objects

Using smart objects enhances layer comps in a few key ways:

➢ Moveable elements like shapes or text remain editable as smart objects when toggled or repositioned.

➢ Apply filters and effects to smart objects non-destructively, then capture all layer states.

➢ Updating a master smart object syncs changes across multiple layer comps.

➢ Reusable smart objects can be shared between comps for efficiency.

CHAPTER EIGHTEEN

Actions

Actions features that allow you to record a series of steps and replay them on any file later. This eliminates the need to manually repeat tasks over and over.

Some examples of how actions can be used include:

> ➤ Batch process edits and effects on multiple photos

➢ Watermarking images

➢ Creating frames or layouts

➢ Applying complex corrections like sharpening or color grading

Learning actions can save you a tremendous amount of time and effort in your creative projects.

Recording Actions in Photoshop

Recording your actions is simple in the Actions panel. Follow these steps:

➢ Open the Actions panel by going to **Window > Actions**.

➢ Click the **"Create new action"** icon at the bottom of the panel.

➢ Name your action and assign a function key shortcut if desired.

➢ Click the **"Record"** button.

➢ Perform the steps you want recorded. This can include edits, effects, and open and save files.

➢ When finished, click the square **"Stop"** button.

➢ The action will now appear in your Actions panel. It has recorded all the steps performed.

Tips for Recording Actions

➢ Work on a sample document that matches the files you will batch process.

➢ Save and close files before stopping recording.

➢ Adjust settings like brush size beforehand.

➢ Record complex steps on separate actions.

➢ Leave the action open if you need to rerecord steps.

Playing Actions

➢ After recording an action, playing it back on any file is very simple.

➢ Open a file you want to run the action on.

➢ Select the action you want to play.

➢ Click the **"Play"** button at the bottom of the Actions panel.

➢ Photoshop will now perform each step in the action automatically.

➢ If the action opens or saves files, dialogue boxes will appear for you to select files. Otherwise, it will play uninterrupted.

➢ You can also play an action on a batch of files using the Batch command, covered later in this guide.

Editing, Deleting, and Managing Actions

The Actions panel gives you full control to manage all your saved actions. Here are some tips:

➢ Reorder actions by dragging them up or down the list.

➢ Delete an action by dragging it to the trash icon.

➢ To edit an action, load the action, click the left-facing arrow to open the steps, make changes, and then click the right-facing arrow to re-collapse it.

➢ To create a new action set, use the top right menu. This helps organize actions.

➤ Toggle the panel menu Recording Options to fine-tune settings.

➤ Taking time to organize and edit your actions will make them easier to use and batch apply.

Batch Processing with Actions

The true power of actions lies in the ability to batch-process edits on multiple files. Here is how:

➤ Go to **File > Automate > Batch**.

➤ Select the action you want to run.

➤ Click **"Choose"** to select a source folder of files.

➤ Check over the destination settings, then click OK.

➤ Photoshop will run the action on each file automatically, saving the output to the destination.

➤ You can also add or skip actions using the Batch dialog. For example, run one action on all files, then run a second action.

Using Conditional Actions

Conditional actions give you even more control over batch processing. They allow you to specify conditions for actions to run.

To create a conditional action:

- ➢ Record the initial action steps as usual.
- ➢ Click the box with a dot next to the action to open conditional options.
- ➢ Choose a condition like file type, layer count, document size, etc.
- ➢ Set the parameters for the condition.
- ➢ Record the steps to perform if the condition is met.
- ➢ Click the box with an X to set the alternative steps if the condition is not met.
- ➢ Record those steps.
- ➢ Now when you batch process, the action will check the conditional parameters on each file and only perform the relevant steps.

Scripts

Scripts allow you to automate repetitive tasks and perform complex functions in Photoshop. Instead of manually repeating actions, you can create or install scripts to speed up your workflow.

Browsing Scripts

Photoshop 2024 comes with a variety of pre-installed scripts you can use right away. Here's how to view them:

➢ Open Photoshop and click **File > Scripts** to open the Scripts menu. This menu contains scripts built into Photoshop.

➢ Click Browse to open the Browse Scripts dialog box. This window contains folders with different script categories like Files, Layers, Math, etc.

➢ Expand a category folder to view the scripts within it. Click a script to see its description at the bottom of the dialog box.

➢ When you find a script you want to use, leave the Browse Scripts dialog box open. You'll run the script from here next.

Installing Scripts

In addition to built-in scripts, you can install free and paid scripts created by third-party developers:

➢ Find scripts created by third-party developers online. Free scripts are available on sites like GitHub or Adobe Add-ons marketplace. Paid scripts can be purchased from sites like Envato Market.

➢ Download the script file(s) to your computer. Scripts usually come as .js or .jsx files.

➢ In Photoshop, click **File > Scripts > Browse** to open the **Browse Scripts** dialog box.

➢ Click the Folder Icon on the top left and choose Install Scripts File.

➢ Navigate to the script file(s) you downloaded and select them to install into Photoshop.

➢ The new scripts will now appear in the designated folders organized by category.

Running Scripts

Once you've identified a script to use, running it is simple:

- ➤ With the script selected in the Browse Scripts dialog box, click Run.
- ➤ Some scripts launch immediately, while others prompt you to configure settings before running. Enter any required information.
- ➤ The script will execute the automated tasks and provide notifications when finished.
- ➤ View your image to see the results. The changes made will depend on the purpose of the script.
- ➤ If needed, you can undo the actions by clicking Edit > Undo or using keyboard shortcuts.

Editing Scripts

With some JavaScript knowledge, you can view and edit existing scripts to better suit your needs:

➤ In the Browse Scripts dialog box, right-click a script and select Edit Source to open it in the ExtendScript Toolkit editor.

➤ Examine the code to understand what the script does. The syntax will be JavaScript/ExtendScript.

➤ To edit, click inside the code editor and make changes as desired. Be careful not to introduce errors.

➤ When finished editing, click the Save icon to overwrite the existing script file.

➤ Rerun the script to see your customized actions.

➤ If your edits cause errors, revert to the original script code and try again.

Image Processor

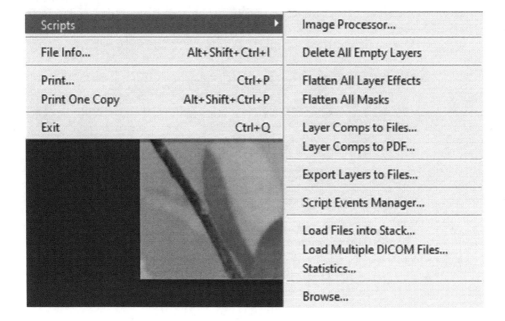

The Image Processor allows you to batch process and convert multiple images at once. You can resize images, save them in different formats, rename files, and adjust other options to automate working with multiple photos.

Saving Formats

> ➤ The Image Processor lets you save batches of files in various formats.

> ➤ Open the images you want to process in Photoshop.

➢ Go to **File > Scripts > Image Processor**. This opens the Image Processor dialog box.

➢ Under Save As, check the file types you want to save the images as. Common options are JPEG, TIFF, PNG, PDF, etc.

➢ For JPEG files, you can enter a Quality setting from 0 to 12 with 12 being the highest quality.

➢ Check the ICC Profile box to preserve color profiles in the exported images.

➢ You can choose to suppress color profile warnings as well.

➢ Click Run to process and save the images in the specified formats.

➢ The reformatted images will be saved in the same location as the originals by default.

Editing Photos

Whether you want to make quick corrections and tweaks or go deep into specialized editing techniques, Photoshop 2024 makes it easy. With a little practice and creativity, you'll be editing pro-quality pictures in no time.

Opening Photos in Photoshop

➢ Open Adobe Photoshop. On a Windows PC, click the Start button then select Photoshop from the list of apps. On a Mac, click the Photoshop app icon in the Dock.

➢ Click **File > Open...** or press Ctrl/Command + O on your keyboard.

➢ In the window that appears, navigate to the photo file you want to open, select it, and click Open.

➢ The photo will now open in Photoshop, ready for editing.

➢ Adjusting Basics: Cropping, Brightness and Contrast

Cropping

One of the most common improvements you can make to any photo is cropping. Cropping allows you to trim away unwanted outer areas of the image and bring the subject into focus.

Here's how to crop an image in Photoshop 2024:

> ➢ Select the Crop tool from the toolbar on the left side of the screen. It looks like a square with the bottom right corner crossed out.

> ➢ Click and drag your mouse cursor to make a cropping box on the part of the image you want to keep.

> ➢ Once satisfied with the crop area, click the checkmark in the options bar at the top to confirm the crop.

> ➢ To adjust or move the crop box, simply click and drag the edges and corners.

> ➢ Use the aspect ratio presets in the options bar to lock the crop into specific proportions like square or 16:9.

Brightness and Contrast

The Brightness and Contrast controls allow you to make your photos sharper and clearer with only a few quick adjustments. Here's how to use them:

> ➢ Select **Layer > New Adjustment Layer > Brightness/Contrast**. This will add an adjustments layer in the Layers panel.
> ➢ In the Properties panel on the right side, drag the Brightness slider right to make the image brighter or left to darken it.
> ➢ Drag the Contrast slider right to increase contrast and make the image pop or left to decrease contrast and make it more flat.
> ➢ Adjust both settings subtly until you achieve the desired look. Beware of going too extreme with the adjustments.

Applying Filters

Photoshop's huge library of filters allows you to add creative effects, color casts, textures, and other enhancements. Here are 5 useful ways to use filters:

➢ **Sharpen -** To add clarity and focus, go to Filter > Sharpen > Unsharp Mask. Adjust the sliders to sharpen the image.

➢ **Black and White -** Remove color and create dramatic B&W photos with Filter > Camera Raw Filter. In the panel, click the B&W tab and adjust the sliders.

➢ **Vintage –** Make a photo look retro and aged by applying the Camera Raw filter, then switching to the Effects tab. Try the Vignette and Grain sliders.

➢ **Blur –** For a soft, dreamy look, select Filter > Blur > Gaussian Blur. Use the slider to control the strength of the blur.

➢ **Noise –** Add film grain texture with Filter > Noise > Add Noise. Adjust the Amount for fine grain or coarse.

Removing Imperfections

➢ Spots, blemishes, and other unwanted elements can easily be removed using

Photoshop's healing tools. Here's how to zap imperfections:

➢ Zoom in close on the area needing retouching.

➢ Select the Spot Healing Brush and adjust the size to just slightly larger than the imperfection.

➢ Click on the imperfection to remove it seamlessly. The Spot Healing brush will sample from surrounding areas to cover it.

➢ For larger areas, use the Healing Brush. Hold Alt/Option and click a good area, then paint over the problem area to blend and match textures.

➢ Use the Patch tool to remove larger objects or regions. Click and drag to select the area, then drag to an area that will blend well and hit Enter/Return.

Combining Photos

Creating photo collages or composites is easy in Photoshop thanks to layers. Follow these simple steps:

➢ Open the two photos you want to combine.

➢ Select all of one photo (Ctrl/Cmd + A) and copy it (Ctrl/Cmd + C).

➢ Click the other photo to select it, then paste (Ctrl/Cmd + V) the first image. It will appear on a new layer above the second photo.

➢ Use the Move tool to slide the pasted photo into position over the base photo.

➢ Right-click the pasted layer and select Blending Options. Play with options like Gradient Overlay to integrate it.

➢ Use layer masks to selectively reveal parts of the bottom layer for a seamless composite.

Getting Creative

With Photoshop 2024, you have endless options for taking your photos from mundane to magical. Here are a few ideas for spicing up your edits using text, shapes, and brushes:

➢ Add inspirational text quotes using the Type tool

➤ Use custom brushes to paint textures or details onto photos

➤ Draw shapes and vectors to add graphics and illustrations

➤ Add watercolor or hand-painted elements using Bristle brush tips

➤ Splatter paint using the Brush tool with Scatter dynamics

➤ Add sparkles and lights with the Brush tool in Dissolve mode

Exporting and Saving

When you're done editing your photo, here's how to save a copy for use online or in print:

➤ Click File > Export > Export As.

➤ Choose a file format like JPEG, PNG, or TIFF. JPEG works for most photos.

➤ Select a quality setting. For online use, medium to high is good. For print, use maximum quality.

➢ Give the exported photo a name and click Save.

➢ Close the original PSD file with all layers intact to preserve your work.

➢ With these Photoshop techniques, you can turn any image into a work of art.

Designing Event Flyers

An eye-catching event flyer is key to promoting your event and driving attendance. In this simple tutorial, we'll go through how to design a professional, custom flyer from scratch on Adobe Photoshop 2024.

Before You Begin

➢ Have the event details on hand - date, time, location, speakers, etc. This will be needed for the flyer content.

➢ Determine the flyer dimensions and orientation. Standard sizes are 8.5" x 11" (letter) or 11" x 17" (tabloid). Orientation can be portrait or landscape.

➢ Decide if the flyer will be printed or digital. Print requires higher resolution.

➢ Gather any brand assets like logos that need to be included.

Creating a New Photoshop File

➢ Open Adobe Photoshop 2024.

➢ Navigate to **File > New**.

➢ Name the file for your event flyer.

➢ Set the width and height according to your desired flyer dimensions.

➢ For print flyers, set the resolution to 300 dpi. For digital, 72 dpi is fine.

➢ Click the color mode drop-down and select RGB Color.

➢ Hit OK.

Designing the Flyer Layout

➢ Grab the Rectangle Shape tool from the toolbar. Use this to map out boxes for flyer elements.

➢ Consider layout principles like alignment, proximity, repetition, and contrast to organize elements.

➢ Use grid guides (View > New Guide Layout) to cleanly align boxes.

Place key text and graphic elements like:

➢ Event Title

➢ High impact image

➢ Date, time, and location

➢ Brief event description

➢ Sponsor logos

➢ Contact information

➢ Play with font sizes, styles, and colors that fit the event aesthetic.

Enhancing the Flyer Visuals

➢ Search Adobe Stock within Photoshop for eye-catching photos relevant to the event.

➢ Drag and drop the chosen photo onto the flyer background layer.

➢ Use the Crop tool to refine the image size and placement as needed.

➢ Use Adjustment Layer effects like Brightness/Contrast, Hue/Saturation, and more to enhance the photo pop.

➢ Add extra design elements like shape graphics, textures, or themed illustrations.

Finishing Touches

➢ Unify imagery and text with color overlays or backgrounds.

➢ Use layer effects like drop shadows, inner shadows, or glows to make elements stand out.

➢ Sharpen important text for legibility.

➢ Add finishing design details.

Exporting the Event Flyer

➢ Navigate to **File > Export > Export As**

➢ Select JPEG or PNG format.

➢ For print, mark the Max Quality checkbox.

➢ Select the desired file location and hit Save.

➢ The custom event flyer is now complete and ready to share.

CONCLUSION

Adobe Photoshop 2024 has taken image editing and graphic design to exciting new levels. With features like one-click subject selection, enhanced Object Removal, improved Generative Fill, and the addition of AI capabilities, Photoshop 2024 makes creative work faster and easier than ever before.

Throughout this guide, we've discovered the software's impressive competencies for editing photos, creating illustrations, designing layouts, and more. Photoshop's layers, filters, adjustment tools, and comprehensive toolbox equip you to produce stunning visuals and graphics.

The new automation features also save you time and effort. With Photoshop 2024, no creative endeavor is out of reach. Experienced users and newcomers alike will find this upgraded version of Photoshop to be an indispensable asset.

Don't hesitate to master Adobe's premier image editing software—download Photoshop 2024 now and unlock your creative potential.

With practice and experimentation, you'll be creating pixel-perfect works of art in no time.

ABOUT THE AUTHOR

Curtis Campbell is an intelligent and innovative computer scientist with experience in software engineering. As a renowned technology expert, his passion for capturing still photos and motion pictures has led him into photography and videography, which he is doing with excellence. Curtis has produced several tutorials on different topics. As a researcher and a prolific writer with proficiency in handling tech products, he learned different approaches to managing issues on the internet and other applications.